NoBODY

except JESUS

by Robert Davis

Almost two thousand years ago, on a hillside outside the city walls
of Jerusalem, three men on three crosses were crucified.
The man nailed to the cross, which stood in the middle was
NoBODY except JESUS
the Son of God.

PublishAmerica
Baltimore

First printing

ISBN: 1-4137-6645-5
PUBLISHED BY PUBLISHAMERICA, LLLP
www.publishamerica.com
Baltimore

Printed in the United States of America

This book is dedicated to
Rob Russel Davis.

Doris;
May God Bless You
and your family.
Thank You
Bob Davis

Acknowledgments

Above all others, I praise the name of our Lord and Savior for everything He has done for us! I am so unworthy!

My wife, Cindy, for her love, encouragement and support. I thank you from the bottom of my heart for believing in me. You truly are a gift to me from God.

Mike Ramey, my good friend and Christian brother, who gave me a laptop computer so I could write this book.

PublishAmerica, I would like to express my appreciation for believing in this manuscript and making my dream a reality.

Contents

Introduction

I believe that all Christians have a responsibility to be sensitive to the spiritual understandings and beliefs of other Christians. In my opinion, there is not a single living Christian who has a complete understanding of all Scripture. The only statement that I will make is this: what is written in the following pages of this book is only my present understanding of God's written Word. I believe with all of my heart that you, the reader, should decide if you believe it to be correct or incorrect. My hope and prayer is for all Christians to act in a compassionate, gentle, loving and Christ-like way. I sincerely pray this for myself, hoping that I will never believe I have no need for any further spiritual growth. I hope and pray that I always have the opinion of myself as being a spiritual babe in Christ. My prayers are for a meek heart and a humble spirit, which will glorify NoBODY except JESUS.

I will be using three Bible translations: the New Revised Standard (NRSV), the New International (NIV) and the King James (KJV). I will also use Strong's *Greek and Hebrew Concordance*. My purpose for writing this book is to attempt to explain the gospel of Jesus Christ and God's plan of salvation in an easy-to-understand way for people like myself. I will briefly share with you my thoughts on Christian maturity. My main desire and goal is to allow Scripture to talk to us and show us the story of conversion and salvation. For this reason, many verses of Scripture will be repeatedly used in attempting to reach this goal.

If you do not enjoy reading Scripture, you may not enjoy reading this book. Another goal of mine is to write this book in a way which will enable the teachings in this book to be used as Bible study lessons. I believe that God has revealed himself to mankind through His Son.

I believe the Bible to be the only inspired written revelation of God given to mankind. I believe that God is still giving illumination, understanding, and spiritual light of His written Word. I sincerely hope and pray that the goals which I desire to reach will be achieved with God's help. To His praise and for the glory of His Son, only.

Terms like *born again, conversion, justification, spiritual circumcision, imputed righteousness* and *baptismal regeneration* were not clear to me for a long time. I truly believe that the gospel of Jesus Christ is simple to understand. It is amazing to me how complicated we have made it. Our intellectual wisdom—the wisdom of man—has complicated the simplicity of preaching Christ crucified. Denominational Christianity in my mind has sadly become Christian division. Divided Christianity is not Christian unity. We waste efforts, energy, time and resources disputing amongst ourselves. Manmade creeds have replaced the simplicity of preaching Christ crucified. I personally do not believe that someone must be a scholar of the Greek language or have a degree in theology to understand God's terms for salvation. You may be asking yourself, How could this be true? Well, I sincerely believe that God, who created man, knows His creation. I believe that God does not want anyone to perish (2 Peter 3:9), and I also sincerely believe that God has infinite wisdom. Therefore I am very confident that God is well aware that the vast majority of individuals would never have these degrees. I personally do not believe that any Christian denomination or individual Christian, whether they be Baptist, Lutheran, Methodist, or of any other denomination, has a completely correct understanding of all Scripture. I believe that the spiritual body of Christ—His spiritual church—is made up of many members from various denominations.

In my mind, I see denominational names being left on this side of the entrance gates of Heaven. I also believe that His church has always existed and I do not believe that any individual throughout history has had to re-establish His church. His church existed before the reformation movement, before the restoration movement, and before any other manmade movement. The power of Light has never been defeated and never will be defeated by Satan or anyone else.

Jesus Christ established His church and said that it would prevail even against the gates of hell. If any person has ever made the claim that they had to re-established His church, then either that person or Jesus was wrong. In my mind, there is no other possible conclusion. No amount of discussion could ever convince me that Jesus was wrong.

And I say also unto thee, That thou art Peter, and upon this rock I will build my church; and the gates of hell shall not prevail against it.

— *KJV, Mat. 16:18*

Over the past centuries Satan has continuously persecuted and attempted to destroy the church. I am certain that Satan is trying harder today than yesterday and I believe that he will try even harder tomorrow than he is today. As days, weeks, months, years and centuries pass; Satan is well aware that his time is coming to an end. As time passes, I believe Satan's desperation must be continuously increasing. This desperation in my mind will without a doubt bring an increase of Satan's efforts to destroy the Church. Satan's time is running out and Satan is well aware of it. Only God knows the exact day of this glorious and wonderful future event. Scripture declares this and we should believe this, regardless of how many individuals believe and have stated that they have figured something out, when Scripture clearly informs us that no man knows except God!

No one knows about that day or hour, not even the angels in heaven, nor the Son, but only the Father. As it was in the days of Noah, so it will be at the coming of the Son of Man.

— *NIV, Mat. 24:36-37*

I have no desire to insult or accuse anyone of anything. I truly believe, however, that all Christians have a responsibility to our Lord to know to the best of their ability what is true and what is false doctrine. We can only fulfill this responsibility by growing spiritually. It seems to me that the vast majority of us were spiritual infants when we first became Christians. Our natural physical maturity at birth was the responsibility of our parents; as newborn infants we, by ourselves, could do nothing to insure our maturity and our survival. We were totally dependent on others. Our spiritual birth, however, is quite a different story. Our spiritual birth and our spiritual maturity are largely dependent on us. Nobody can force us to believe, nobody can make us grow spiritually, and nobody can make us a member of the body of Christ, His spiritual church. We need nobody;

Nobody, except Jesus.

Nobody means no man-written creed, no man-made ordinance, no man-made law, no man-performed ritual, nobody: Nobody, except Jesus! Our salvation is a gift from God. Why? To insure that nobody could ever boast. Nobody means nobody, you, me or any other Christian throughout all of history.

For the wages of sin is death; but the gift of God is eternal life through Jesus Christ our Lord.
— KJV, Rom. 6:23

For by grace are ye saved through faith; and that not of yourselves: it is the gift of God.
— KJV, Eph. 2:8

Not of works, lest any man should boast.
— KJV, Eph. 2:9

Nobody is righteous, not even one.

As it is written, There is none righteous, no, not one.
— KJV, Rom. 3:10

Nobody can earn their righteousness with any act or any amount of works, no matter how righteous their deeds or works may be.

For all have sinned, and come short of the glory of God;
— KJV, Rom. 3:23

This is not from men; this is what God has clearly declared. I once heard a saying; "If we could work our way to Heaven, we would brag our way to hell." How true! Our spiritual maturity is very different from our physical development and maturity. We need the gentle and loving care of spiritually mature Christians to encourage, guide and help us with our spiritual growth and maturity. It is their responsibility to help us mature spiritually. We, ourselves, as Christians, however, have an even greater responsibility to Christ to grow and mature spiritually. Other Christians, whether they are friends, parents, Sunday school teachers, pastors or ministers, are unable to do it for us. Christians must ask themselves: *Will I be committed to God? Am I fulfilling my responsibilities to God?* Your desire and the efforts you make towards spiritual maturity are decisions which belong to nobody except you! You are the only one, who can make these decisions.

When I think of the pain and suffering that Jesus endured for my sins, I realize that I am personally responsible for His unimaginable painful crucifixion and death. I imagine His precious blood pouring out of His wounds for the sole purpose of covering my numerous sins. I tell myself, "You are responsible for His death! You should then be responsible to mature spiritually 'for or because' this is His will." I am ashamed and also totally embarrassed when I recall how much precious time I wasted after I became a Christian. How many precious years I foolishly wasted away, showing no spiritual growth, bearing no spiritual fruit. Precious time forever lost! How could I have been so foolish, so insensitive, so selfish and so irresponsible? A question with no justifiable answer. I look to the ground, full of shame. So unworthy am I! Nobody has the ability to change the past, we can, however, learn from the past. We should also make the necessary changes, which will insure our continuous future growth and our never-ending spiritual maturity.

Desire, in my opinion, is needed for spiritual maturity. I believe this to be true for the simple reason that without desire, no personal efforts or works would ever follow. Commitment, however, is totally dependent on desire. The greater the desire is, the greater the commitment should be. The greater the commitment, the greater the efforts will be. Desire, commitment and efforts, in my mind, are dependent on something else. It is a word, which means everything. It is a word, which is capable of changing lives forever more. In Greek, the word is *agape*; in English, the word is love. Our personal love for Jesus Christ.

The more we love Jesus, the more we should be committed to Him. The more we love Jesus, the more willing we should be to spiritually crucify the sinful ways of the flesh every single day. The more we spiritually crucify our sinful ways, the more we die to self, living every day for Christ. The more we live for Christ, the more we mature spiritually. The more we mature spiritually, the more Christ-like we become. The more Christ-like we become, the more His Light is seen by others. The greater the numbers are who see and come to Christ, the greater Christ is glorified! In my opinion, this should be the goal of every Christian: to live our lives glorifying;

Nobody, except Jesus!

The help and spiritual food, which we receive from other Christians, is very important; however, I believe that prayer is second to none. I have found over the years that obedience and prayer are the most important elements for successful spiritual growth and Christian maturity. My prayers are for all Christians everywhere to realize the same. The power of prayer in my present understanding is effective only when our actions and our motives are only to glorify Christ and not self! Our actions and the words which we speak are not the only things to be concerned with. We also have the additional responsibility of disciplining even our thoughts. Unfortunately, it was a very long time before I realized this. As I grew spiritually, I began to see my thoughts in a different kind of light.

Casting down imaginations, and every high thing that exalteth itself against the knowledge of God, and bringing into captivity every thought to the obedience of Christ.

— *KJV, 2Cor. 10:5*

But I say unto you, That whosoever looketh on a woman to lust after her hath committed adultery with her already in his heart.

— *KJV, Mat. 5:28*

For my thoughts are not your thoughts, neither are your ways my ways, saith the Lord. For as the heavens are higher than the earth, so are my ways higher than your ways, and my thoughts than your thoughts.

— *KJV, Isa. 55:8-9*

"Easy to be a good Christian," I once foolishly believed, only to be shown the foolishness of me. Spiritual understanding is spiritual light; spiritual light, when received, should bear spiritual fruit.

Chapter 1

His Love

My present understanding of God's will and desire for mankind is that it all started with God's love towards us and will always continue to be His love. God's love is so great and merciful that God's will and desire is that nobody should perish, no matter how great his or her sins may be. His gracious unmerited love is for anyone and everyone. God's love sent His Son to us and for us. God's love existed before time began. God's love created time for man, just as God's love created man. In the beginning, God offered man to eat from the tree of life, man chose to eat from the tree of knowledge. God has given us everything, even time.

I believe that everyone needs to honestly ask themselves how much time are they personally willing to give to God. Our answer to this question is very important to our spiritual maturity. If the total amount of time we decide to give to God is one hour a week on Sunday morning, then we will continue to be spiritually immature Christians, or Christian infants. We will only be able to digest spiritual milk instead of spiritual meat.

For every one that useth milk is unskillful in the word of righteousness: for he is a babe. But strong meat belongeth to them that are of full age, even those who by reason of use have their senses exercised to discern both good and evil.

— KJV, Heb. 5:13-14

If we remain spiritual infants, we will be very limited in our ability to serve our precious Lord and Savior. Nobody can make this decision for us; again this is our own personal decision. The more we love Him, the more time we should be willing to give to Him; in worship, in fellowship, studying, in prayer, in witnessing and serving Him in any possible way. True love requires many things. Without time, it is impossible for love to grow and mature. True love is a willingness to make sacrifices for the sole benefit and good of others. Unselfish love truly is very precious. I believe love is more precious than time. I once thought of the word eternity; I soon realized that nobody in eternity will be walking around with a watch or looking for a clock. There will be no need to watch the hands of time in eternity.

We make time for the things, which are most important and precious to us in this life. Where we place our desires, is where our priorities will be. Commitment, efforts, resources and time are given to our priorities. We either love the things of this world and ourselves or we express and show our love for Jesus and live to glorify and to serve Him. I truly believe the more we love God, the more time we give to Him. Nobody can serve two masters. We either live to serve Christ or we live to serve self.

Decisions, decisions, decisions... life is full of them. No way to avoid them, however, the most important decision made by any individual in life is: Do I personally believe Jesus Christ was crucified for my sins? How are we brought to this question? By preaching and by hearing the gospel of Christ. "That Christ died for our sins."

Now, brothers, I want to remind you of the gospel I preached to you, which you received and on which you have taken your stand. By this gospel you are saved, if you hold firmly to the word I preached to you. Otherwise, you have believed in vain. For what I received I passed on to you as of first importance: that Christ died for our sins according to the Scriptures.

— NIV, 1 Cor. 15:1-3

How, then, can they call on the one they have not believed in? And how can they believe in the one of whom they have not heard? And how can they hear without someone preaching to them?

— NIV, Rom. 10:14

I personally prefer the words teaching and witnessing instead of the word preaching. I believe with all of my heart and soul that witnessing is a responsibility of all Christians. All Christians are called to witness and therefore to be a minister to others, especially to non-believers. In my mind, there are only two kinds of people in the world: saved and unsaved. We are either a child of God, walking in His Light, or we are walking in spiritual darkness and being deceived by Satan. However, we are all sinners. Christians are saved sinners and non-Christians are unsaved sinners. Some Christians may sin less than some non-Christians. However, in all honesty, one should never deny the possibility that some Christians may sin more than some non-Christians! The distinction between saved and unsaved people, however, is Jesus Christ. This was made possible by a special kind of love. God's gracious unmerited love is for you and for me.

But God commendeth his love[1] toward us, in that, while we were yet sinners, Christ died for us.

— KJV, Rom. 5:8

It all started with a special kind of love: Agape: God's love. The very first verse of Scripture which I memorized as a little child in Sunday school was John 3:16.

For God so loved the world, that he gave his only begotten Son, that whosoever believeth in him should not perish, but have everlasting life.

— KJV, John 3:16.

In the beginning was the Word, and the Word was with God, and the Word was God.

— KJV, John 1:1

And the Word was made flesh, and dwelt among us, (and we beheld his glory, the glory as of the only begotten of the Father), full of grace and truth.

— *KJV, John 1:14*

The word "full" in this verse (John 1:14) is translated from the Greek word *"pleres"* which means full or complete. To paraphrase the above verses: The Word was God and the Word was made flesh. Jesus was God in the flesh revealing Himself to man. Through His Son, we see the glory of God, His complete grace and "full" or complete truth. Complete grace and complete truth, both shown to man, by God, through His Son. A divine level or measure of both grace and of truth, so full and so complete that there is no level or measure any greater. A grace so complete that nobody could ever possibly exceed the grace or the truth expressed and shown by God, to man. God's grace truly is second to none!

For if, when we were enemies, we were reconciled to God by the death of his Son, much more, being reconciled, we shall be saved by his life.

— *KJV, Rom. 5:10*

God's reason or purpose for revealing himself to mankind was that He wanted to reconcile us to Himself. When did God reconcile us? "When we were enemies." How did God do this? "By the death of his Son." These few verses begin to shine spiritual light in a world of spiritual darkness, the spiritual darkness of man, man's lack of spiritual understanding. The light given in these verses by His Light is simple to understand. To paraphrase the above verse: When we were enemies, we were reconciled to God. How? "By the death of His Son," which occurred almost two thousand years ago!

It started with love: God's love for us. A love so amazing, so great and so pure that words are unable to fully express how precious His love really is. Totally unmerited and full of His amazing grace. A gracious righteous love full of unmerited mercy. Complete grace. May we always praise His name! A love so full of His unmerited mercy, it truly is Amazing Grace! How many of us can honestly say that we love our enemies? That we would be willing to do all that we could do for their benefit only, without any gain for ourselves? That we would be willing to die for them? Well, this is exactly what God has already done for each and everyone of us. Unmerited mercy and His complete grace: God loved us before we loved Him. When I think of this, I ask myself the following question: Will I ever in my lifetime, be capable of this kind of love? My shameful answer is always: "I do not think so." This is what the Apostle Paul also wrote in his Epistle to the Ephesians.

And that he might reconcile both unto God in one body by the cross, having slain the enmity thereby.

— KJV, Eph. 2:16

"Might reconcile both unto God." The word "both" refers to Jewish people and Gentiles. "in one body" refers to His spiritual body: His Church. How did "he"(Jesus) do this? "By the cross" and by slaying the "enmity" or hostility? No more separation and no more hostility. All people would now have an opportunity to be the people of God.

And came and preached peace to you which were afar off, and to them that were nigh.

— KJV, Eph. 2:17

"You which were afar off," refers to Gentiles and "them that were nigh" refers to God's chosen people, the Jews. Peace to Gentiles, and peace to Jews; peace to all mankind. Why did Jesus preach peace between God and man? This is why Jesus preached peace. All people, both Jews and Gentiles, were reconciled to God by the cross!

The hostility between Jews and Gentiles and the hostility between God and men was slain by the cross. The atonement had been made and the ransom had been paid! Together all people could now be the people of God, in one body: His spiritual Church. This was accomplished almost two thousand years ago by: Nobody, except Jesus. However, with this privilege: A personal decision would have to be made!

Chapter 2

The First Covenant

[19] When Moses had proclaimed every commandment of the law to all the people, he took the blood of calves, together with water, scarlet wool and branches of hyssop, and sprinkled the scroll and all the people. [20] He said, "This is the blood of the covenant, which God has commanded you to keep." [21] In the same way, he sprinkled with the blood both the tabernacle and everything used in its ceremonies. [22] In fact, the law requires that nearly everything be cleansed with blood, and without the shedding of blood there is no forgiveness. [23] It was necessary, then, for the copies of the heavenly things to be.

— NIV, Heb. 9:19 23

[1] Now the first covenant had regulations for worship and also an earthly sanctuary. [2] A tabernacle was set up. In its first room were the lampstand, the table and the consecrated bread; this was called the Holy Place. [3] Behind the second curtain was a room called the Most Holy Place, [4] which had the golden altar of incense and the gold-covered ark of the covenant. This ark contained the gold jar of manna, Aaron's staff that had budded, and the stone tablets of the covenant. [5] Above the ark were the cherubim of the Glory, overshadowing the atonement cover. But we cannot discuss these things in detail now. [6] When everything had been arranged like this, the priests entered regularly into the outer room to carry on their ministry. [7] But only the high priest entered the inner room, and that only once a year, and never

without blood, which he offered for himself and for the sins the people had committed in ignorance. [8] The Holy Spirit was showing by this that the way into the Most Holy Place had not yet been disclosed as long as the first tabernacle was still standing. [9] This is an illustration for the present time, indicating that the gifts and sacrifices being offered were not able to clear the conscience of the worshiper. [10] They are only a matter of food and drink and various ceremonial washings—external regulations applying until the time of the new order.

— NIV, Heb. 9:1-10

[1] The law is only a shadow of the good things that are coming—not the realities themselves. For this reason it can never, by the same sacrifices repeated endlessly year after year, make perfect those who draw near to worship. [2] If it could, would they not have stopped being offered? For the worshipers would have been cleansed once for all, and would no longer have felt guilty for their sins. [3] But those sacrifices are an annual reminder of sins, [4] because it is impossible for the blood of bulls and goats to take away sins.

— NIV, Heb. 10:1-4

Day after day every priest stands and performs his religious duties; again and again he offers the same sacrifices, which can never take away sins.

— NIV, Heb. 10:11

From these verses in the Book of Hebrews, we receive some understanding of the first covenant. Let's take a brief look at these verses. In the tabernacle behind the second curtain was a room called the Most Holy Place. In this room were a golden altar and the gold-covered ark, which contained the gold jar of manna, Aaron's staff and also the stone tablets, which Moses had received from God. Above the ark were the cherubim of the Glory, which overshadowed the atonement cover. The priests of the tabernacle were not permitted to enter the Most Holy Place. Only the High Priest could enter into the Most Holy Place.

Once a year, the High Priest would purify himself by ritual ceremonies and ritual washings and could only then, enter with the shed blood of innocent animals. The High Priest would offer this blood as atonement for his sins and also for the sins of the people. The law required that nearly everything was to be cleansed or purified with blood. Without the shedding of blood, there was no forgiveness of sins. The Holy Spirit was showing the people of God that the way into the Most Holy Place was not yet available to man. This was done to show and teach God's people that these sacrifices would never be able to change their feelings towards sin.

The people continued to sin year after year and continued to make the same sacrifices year after year "for" or "because" of their sins. The people had no guilt feelings for their sins, nor any guilt for the shed blood of the innocent animals. They continued to sin; their actions continued to be the same. It was also impossible for the blood of bulls and goats to take away their sins. The blood of animals could never cleanse their conscience. In other words, this blood meant nothing to them and had no power to change their minds and their actions. These rituals were to teach and lead God's people to the cleansing power of the precious blood, which would be shed for the forgiveness, or remission of their sins. These rituals would lead them to the Lamb of God; they would lead them to: Nobody, except Jesus!

So the law was put in charge to lead us to Christ that we might be justified by faith.

— NIV, Gal. 3:24

[25] *God presented him as a sacrifice of atonement, through faith in his blood. He did this to demonstrate his justice, because in his forbearance he had left the sins committed beforehand unpunished—* [26] *he did it to demonstrate his justice at the present time, so as to be just and the one who justifies those who have faith in Jesus.*

— NIV, Rom. 3:25-26

Ritual purification! Did water have anything to do with spiritual cleanliness or spiritual purification for the Jewish people (Heb. 9:10)? If so, were these water purification rituals requirements of the Laws of Moses? We will begin our search with the instructions given by God to Moses for the building of the Tabernacle.

A Sanctuary:

⁸ And let them make me a sanctuary; that I may dwell among them. ⁹ According to all that I show thee, after the pattern of the tabernacle, and the pattern of all the instruments thereof, even so shall ye make it.

— KJV, Exo. 25:8-9

A Brass Laver:

¹⁷ And the LORD spake unto Moses, saying, ¹⁸ Thou shalt also make a laver of brass, and his foot also of brass, to wash withal: and thou shalt put it between the tabernacle of the congregation and the altar, and thou shalt put water therein.

— KJV, Exo. 30:17 - 18

And he made the laver of brass, and the foot of it of brass, of the looking glasses of the women assembling, which assembled at the door of the tabernacle of the congregation.

— KJV, Exo. 38:8

A basin or "laver of brass," had a "foot" or base which was also made of brass. A brass laver and its base were both made from the brass of the mirrors of the women. The brass laver was to be placed between the tabernacle and the altar, which was for the burnt offering. Water was to be placed in this brass laver.

The Priesthood:

God chose Aaron and his four sons for the office of the High priesthood.

25

And take thou unto thee Aaron thy brother, and his sons with him, from among the children of Israel, that he may minister unto me in the priest's office, even Aaron, Nadab and Abihu, Eleazar and Ithamar, Aaron's sons.
— *KJV, Exo. 28:1*

We will now look at the preparations for their consecration and also the garments for the High Priest:

And thou shalt make holy garments for Aaron thy brother for glory and for beauty.
— *KJV, Exo. 28:2*

The instructions given by God to Moses for Aaron's holy garments are recorded in Exodus 28:2-39.

And the holy garments of Aaron shall be his sons' after him, to be anointed therein, and to be consecrated in them.
— *KJV, Exo. 29:29*

These holy garments, which were to be worn by the High Priest, were also to be given to the next High Priest.

Garments for the Priests:
And for Aaron's sons thou shalt make coats, and thou shalt make for them girdles, and bonnets shalt thou make for them, for glory and for beauty.
— *KJV, Exo. 28:40*

Aaron and his sons must wear them whenever they enter the Tent of Meeting or approach the altar to minister in the Holy Place, so that they will not incur guilt and die. "This is to be a lasting ordinance for Aaron and his descendants."
— *NIV, Exo. 28:43*

Preparation for the consecration ceremony:
¹ This is what you are to do to consecrate them, so they may serve me as priests: Take a young bull and two rams without defect. ² And from fine wheat flour, without yeast, make bread, and cakes mixed with oil, and wafers spread with oil. ³ Put them in a basket and present them in it—along with the bull and the two rams. ⁴ Then bring Aaron and his sons to the entrance to the Tent of Meeting and wash them with water.

— NIV, Exo. 29:1-4

God gave these instructions to Moses for the purpose of consecrating Aaron and his sons for the priesthood. "From fine wheat flour" Moses was to "make bread, and cakes mixed with oil, and wafers spread with oil." The bread, the cakes and the wafers were to be placed "in a basket." This basket, "a young bull and two rams without defect" along with Aaron and his sons were to be taken by Moses to the entrance to the Tent of Meeting. The very first thing, which was to be done to Aaron and his sons, was that Moses was to "wash them with water."

This consecration ceremony is recorded in Leviticus 7:35 through 8:36. The ceremony was very complicated and there is no reason to go into any further detail. I only wish to show that water was used as an agent in this ancient Jewish consecration ceremony, as demonstrated in Lev. 8:6. And Moses brought Aaron and his sons, and washed them with water.

This washing with water was for the spiritual purification of Aaron and his sons for the priesthood. These instructions were most definitely part of the written Laws of Moses. Exodus 29:4 reads: "wash them with water" and Leviticus 8:6 reads: "washed them with water." This may lead someone to believe that Aaron and his sons were to be completely bathed in water. I honestly believe that no individual has the right to use only bits and pieces of Scripture when they are attempting to support their beliefs. Scripture, in my opinion, should be viewed as completely as possible.

I believe that we should look at Scripture like the pieces of a puzzle and then sincerely put forth our very best efforts to understand as many of the pieces of Scripture as possible. The beauty of any puzzle is the picture which it creates. The beauty is only complete when all of the pieces of that puzzle are correctly in place. If we are missing some of the pieces of the puzzle or have misplaced some of the pieces, then its complete and true beauty is forever lost, never to be seen and never to be realized. I believe that Scripture is the same, the more pieces we have and correctly understand, the more beautiful Scripture becomes to us.

The beauty of God's merciful grace is only known by understanding the fullness of God's love and realizing the total completeness of God's grace. The more we realize how precious the Lamb of God is to us, the more we should glorify Jesus. This being realized, we must take a closer look at Scripture for any additional information concerning this laver and the washing of the Priests. The measurements and size of this laver are not available. However, we are informed that the brass, which was used to make this laver and the base which it was placed on, was made from mirrors of the women. It would seem reasonable to me that this laver was limited in its size. The following verses also provide some additional information for us.

[17] And the LORD spake unto Moses, saying, [18] Thou shalt also make a laver of brass, and his foot also of brass, to wash withal: and thou shalt put it between the tabernacle of the congregation and the altar, and thou shalt put water therein. [19] For Aaron and his sons shall wash their hands and their feet thereat: [20] When they go into the tabernacle of the congregation, they shall wash with water, that they die not; or when they come near to the altar to minister, to burn offering made by fire unto the LORD: [21] So they shall wash their hands and their feet, that they die not: and it shall be a statute for ever to them, even to him and to his seed throughout their generations.

— KJV, Exo. 30:17-21

These few verses inform us that the Priests were to wash their hands and their feet. The fact that this laver was made from the brass of mirrors and was also to be used by the Priests for the washing or cleansing of their hands and feet, are reasons to believe that it was not necessary for this laver to be large in size. What is important is the historical fact that water was used as an agent for the daily spiritual purification of Aaron and his sons. If they went into the tabernacle or near the altar without first washing with water, they would die! This consecration ceremony and the traditional Jewish requirement for spiritual purification by water are very important.

This is the picture, which I have in my mind, of the tabernacle and courtyard.

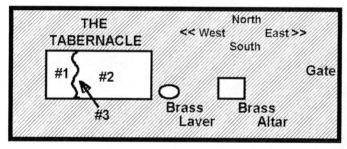

#1. Holy of Holies
#2. Holy Place
#3. The Curtain or Veil

From the above verses, we should be able to realize that Moses was instructed by God to take Aaron and his sons to the brass laver, which was placed between the tabernacle and the brass altar. Moses was to wash their hands and their feet with water from this brass laver, to consecrate them (Exo. 29: 4). Aaron and his sons were also required to wash at this laver, every day before they entered the tabernacle and also before they went to the brass altar (Exo. 30:20). If we search Scripture, we will realize that water has always played a very important role in the Jewish tradition of spiritual purification and was most definitely a part of the Laws of Moses.

What about the purification of the Levites? The Levites were given the responsibility of taking care of the tabernacle. Were water purification rituals also required by God for their holy service? If so, was it required for their spiritual purification?

Purification of the Levites:
⁵ The LORD said to Moses: ⁶ "Take the Levites from among the other Israelites and make them ceremonially clean. ⁷ To purify them, do this: Sprinkle the water of cleansing on them; then have them shave their whole bodies and wash their clothes, and so purify themselves.

— NIV, Num. 8:5 - 7

This separation of the Levites, and this Jewish ceremonial purification ritual for the Levites, was necessary for their services and work pertaining to the tabernacle and are recorded in Numbers 8:5 - 22. This purification ritual was very complicated and my only goal is for us to realize that water was used as an agent for spiritual cleansing. In these few verses, we are informed that Moses was instructed by God to make the Levites ceremonially clean and to purify them. How? "Sprinkle the water of cleansing on them." Sprinkling the Levites with "the water of cleansing" was also part of the Laws of Moses. These requirements were not manmade; these requirements were declared and given by God to Moses.

What was; "the water of cleansing"? Where was Moses to get this: "water of cleansing" to purify the Levites? To receive any additional light on this subject will be necessary to take a close look at the sacrifice of the red heifer. The purpose or reasons for this ritual sacrifice are recorded in the Book of Numbers.

The Red Heifer
¹ The LORD said to Moses and Aaron: ² "This is a requirement of the law that the LORD has commanded: Tell the Israelites to bring you

a red heifer without defect or blemish and that has never been under a yoke. ³ Give it to Eleazar the priest; it is to be taken outside the camp and slaughtered in his presence. ⁴ Then Eleazar the priest is to take some of its blood on his finger and sprinkle it seven times toward the front of the Tent of Meeting. ⁵ While he watches, the heifer is to be burned—its hide, flesh, blood and offal. ⁶ The priest is to take some cedar wood, hyssop and scarlet wool and throw them onto the burning heifer. ⁷ After that, the priest must wash his clothes and bathe himself with water. He may then come into the camp, but he will be ceremonially unclean till evening. ⁸ The man who burns it must also wash his clothes and bathe with water, and he too will be unclean till evening. ⁹ A man who is clean shall gather up the ashes of the heifer and put them in a ceremonially clean place outside the camp. They shall be kept by the Israelite community for use in the water of cleansing; it is for purification from sin. ¹⁰ The man who gathers up the ashes of the heifer must also wash his clothes, and he too will be unclean till evening. This will be a lasting ordinance both for the Israelites and for the aliens living among them."

— NIV, Num. 19:1-10

From these verses we are informed that God told Moses and Aaron to tell the Israelites to bring to them a red heifer, one without any blemish and also which had never had a yoke placed upon it. They (Moses and Aaron) were to give this red heifer to Eleazar the priest. This red heifer was to be taken outside of the camp and slaughtered in the presence of Eleazar. Eleazar was to place some of the blood from this red heifer upon his finger and then sprinkle it seven times towards the front of the Tent of Meeting. Now this next part may be a little hard, if not impossible, for us to understand, however, this is what is written in the text. The hide, flesh, blood and offal (dung) were to be burnt. While Eleazar watched the burning of this red heifer, he was to "take some cedar wood, hyssop and scarlet wool and throw them onto the burning heifer." After that, the priest must wash his clothes and bathe himself with water. He could then come into the camp, but he would be ceremonially unclean till evening.

Also, the man who burns it must also wash his clothes and bathe with water, and he too will be unclean till evening. Then, a man who was clean was to gather up the ashes of the heifer and put them in a ceremonially clean place outside the camp. The ashes were to be kept by the Israelite community for use in the water of cleansing; it would be for purification from sin. Then, the man who gathered up the ashes of the heifer must also wash his clothes, and he too would be unclean till evening. This was to be a lasting ordinance both for the Israelites and for the aliens living among them.

From these verses we have learned that one reason for the sacrifice of the red heifer was that Moses and the Israelites were instructed by God to use the ashes from the burning of the red heifer in water. This water of cleansing was to be used:

1. For purification from sin by the Israelites:
⁹ A man who is clean shall gather up the ashes of the heifer and put them in a ceremonially clean place outside the camp. They shall be kept by the Israelite community for use in the water of cleansing; it is for purification from sin. ¹⁰ The man who gathers up the ashes of the heifer must also wash his clothes, and he too will be unclean till evening. This will be a lasting ordinance both for the Israelites and for the aliens living among them.
                                                        — NIV, Num. 19:9 - 10

2. For ceremonial cleansing; consecration of the Levites:
⁵ The LORD said to Moses: ⁶ "Take the Levites from among the other Israelites and make them ceremonially clean. ⁷ To purify them do this: Sprinkle the water of cleansing on them: then have them shave their whole bodies and wash their clothes, and so purify themselves.
                                                        — NIV, Num. 8:5 - 7

3. For purification of uncleanness:
¹¹ Whoever touches the dead body of anyone will be unclean for seven days. ¹² He must purify himself with the water on the third day and on the seventh day; then he will be clean. But if he does not purify himself on the third and seventh days, he will not be

clean. [13] *Whoever touches the dead body of anyone and fails to purify himself defiles the Lord's tabernacle. That person must be cut off from Israel. Because the water of cleansing has not been sprinkled on him, he is unclean; his uncleanness remains on him.*
— *NIV, Num. 19:11 - 13*

It may be helpful to realize that the tabernacle and all of its furnishings were made to be transportable during the forty years of wandering in the desert. If we continue our search to the time of the building of the Temple by Solomon, we receive more information concerning what is referred to as a molten sea made of brass, which replaced the brass laver, when Solomon had the first Temple built.

And he made a molten sea, ten cubits from the one brim to the other: it was round all about, and his height was five cubits: and a line of thirty cubits did compass it round about.
— *KJV, 1 Ki. 7:23*

A cubit is about eighteen inches. Ten cubits would be fifteen feet for the diameter. Five cubits would be seven and a half feet for the height. Thirty cubits would be forty-five feet for the circumference. According to the Holman's Bible Dictionary for Windows, "The estimated weight is about 30 tons and the estimated volume is about 12,000 gallons (U.S.). The basin was used for the purification of the priests (2 Chr. 4:6)." If we search for additional information concerning this molten sea, we discover a discrepancy when we compare the following verses.

It was a handbreadth in thickness, and its rim was like the rim of a cup, like a lily blossom. It held two thousand baths.
— *NIV, 1Ki. 7:26*

It was a handbreadth in thickness, and its rim was like the rim of a cup, like a lily blossom. It held three thousand baths.
— *NIV, 2 Chr. 4:5*

I was never aware of this discrepancy until very recently. I believe that the original signed manuscripts were flawless. However, we must realize that the originals do not exist and we have only manmade copies of the originals. Two thousand or three thousand baths, which ever one is correct, is of no importance to me. My only desire is to show; that this molten sea of brass was used for ritual purification washings by the Priests (2 Chr. 4:6). The size of this molten sea of brass was enormous.

If we take a look at some verses in the Book of Hebrews, we find that the writer of Hebrews, thought by many scholars to be the Apostle Paul, refers to these water purification rituals as; "various ceremonial washings — external regulations" (NIV), "divers washings, and carnal ordinances" (KJV) and "various baptisms" (NRSV). This verse (Heb. 9:10) is a direct reference to the washings or immersions, which were required under the old covenant (Lev. 16:4) for the High Priest on the Day of Atonement.

They are only a matter of food and drink and various ceremonial washings—external regulations applying until the time of the new order.
— *NIV, Heb. 9:10*

Which stood only in meats and drinks, and divers washings, and carnal ordinances, imposed on them until the time of reformation.
— *KJV, Heb. 9:10*

but deal only with food and drink and various baptisms, regulations for the body imposed until the time comes to set things right.
— *NRSV, Heb. 9:10*

It is very important for us to realize that the word; "washings" in Heb. 9:10 (KJV) is translated from the Greek word baptismos.

Strong's Concordance:
G909 baptismos, bap-tis-mos';
from G907; ablution (cerem. or Chr.): baptism, washing.

We are also informed in the ninth chapter of Hebrews and also in the twenty-fourth chapter of Exodus (24:4 - 8) that when the people of Israel had agreed (Exo. 24:7) to obey God's laws (the Mosaic Laws), Moses sprinkled them with blood and water to consecrate them (Heb. 9:19).

[19] When Moses had proclaimed every commandment of the law to all the people, he took the blood of calves, together with water, scarlet wool and branches of hyssop, and sprinkled the scroll and all the people. [20] He said, "This is the blood of the covenant, which God has commanded you to keep." [21] In the same way, he sprinkled with the blood both the tabernacle and everything used in its ceremonies. [22] In fact, the law requires that nearly everything be cleansed with blood, and without the shedding of blood there is no forgiveness.

— NIV, Heb. 9:19 - 22

Realizing that blood and water were required under the Mosaic Laws for both Jewish purification and consecration rituals, it may then be easier for us to have a better understanding of difficult verses like:

who have been chosen according to the foreknowledge of God the Father, through the sanctifying work of the Spirit, for obedience to Jesus Christ and sprinkling by his blood: Grace and peace be yours in abundance

— NIV, 1 Peter 1:2

We were not literally or physically sprinkled with His blood. We were spiritually cleansed, spiritually purified, spiritually washed, spiritually sprinkled with His blood, through faith in His blood for the remission of sins. I have no desire to go any deeper with this topic. My only goal was to allow God's written word to inform and teach us that water purification rituals were both required and practiced under the Laws of Moses. It is easy to understand why Peter referred to the Laws of Moses as "a yoke that neither we nor our fathers have been able to bear" (Acts 15:10).

Purification by water was also required "when a man has an emission of semen, he must bathe his whole body with water, and he will be unclean till evening" (Lev. 15:16). And "when a man lies with a woman and there is an emission of semen, both must bathe with water and they will be unclean till evening" (NIV, Lev. 15:18).

Water purification rituals and sacrifices of any kind for atonement were to be discontinued. These water purification rituals and atonement sacrifices had symbolized the cleansing, washing or purification which would be provided by Christ. They were to teach and lead the Israelites and us to nobody; Nobody, except Jesus (Gal. 3:24). Being aware of these required Jewish atonement and water purification rituals is absolutely necessary if we truly desire to understand their symbolic representation of Christ and the precious blood of the sacrificial Lamb of God.

The tabernacle, or in later times the Temple, was a worldly sanctuary (Heb. 9:1) built by the hands of man (Heb. 8:2), symbolizing what is in heaven. The representation of Christ as our High Priest was also represented in the Mosaic Law by the high priest entering into the Holy of Holies once a year on the Day of Atonement (Heb. 9:1–7). The required ritual sacrifices were symbolic of the future sacrificial Lamb of God (John 1:29) and the blood of these sacrifices (Heb. 10:4) used by the high priest for atonement on this day was also symbolic of His precious blood. It was impossible for the blood of bulls and goats to take away sins (Heb. 10:4). The bodies of these sacrifices were burnt outside of the camp (Heb. 13:11) also representing that Christ would suffer outside the city gates of Jerusalem (Heb. 13:12).

On that special holy day (the Day of Atonement), the high priest was required to wash his flesh in water (Lev. 16:4), symbolizing spiritual purification. The reason for this act of spiritual purification by water was that the required garments the high priest was required to wear when entering into the Holy of Holies on the Day of Atonement were holy garments (Lev. 16:4), which symbolized the purity, holiness and the sinless righteousness of Christ, who would be the future High Priest of a new and better covenant (Heb. 8:6). Water being the physical element, which physically removes the filth of the flesh, (Lev. 16:4) was a symbolic example of His precious blood, which spiritually cleanses the body, preparing the body to wear holy garments or a new spotless white robe.

This act of spiritual purification by water also symbolized the necessity of spiritual cleanliness before one can be clothed with the imputed righteousness (Rom. 4:24) of Christ, having our robes washed by his blood (Rev. 7:14) This act of spiritual purification by water for the high priest symbolized the future spiritual purification from sins by the precious blood of Christ, which is also symbolically referred to as; "clean water" in Ezek. 36:25 and "pure water" in Heb. 10:22 (KJV).

On the Day of Atonement, the high priest would enter into the Holy of Holies with the blood of the sacrificed bull and with his finger he would sprinkle the sacrificial blood on the front (the eastward-side) and also before the mercy seat seven times, making atonement for his sins (Lev. 16:14). After making this atonement for his sins with blood, the high priest would exit the Holy of Holies and return with the sacrificial blood for the people. The high priest would sprinkle the sacrificial blood for the sins of the people on the front and also before the mercy seat seven times, making atonement for the sins of the Israelites (Lev. 16:15-17). The Holy of Holies was a man-made symbolic representation of a greater and more perfect tabernacle (Heb. 9:11) heaven itself (Heb. 9:24).

The high priest was a symbolic representation of Christ, our High Priest (Heb. 8:1). The high priest entering by the blood of the sacrificial bull was a symbolic representation of Christ (Heb. 9:9) entering heaven's Holy of Holies by His own blood (Heb. 9:12). The sacrificial blood sprinkled on the mercy seat for the atonement of the people (Lev. 16:15 - 17) was a symbolic representation of the future and now present atoning, redeeming (Mat. 26:28 and 1 Pet. 1:18 - 19) cleansing and washing (Heb. 10:19 - 22) that the blood of Christ has provided

ROBERT DAVIS

for all who believe and repent. Examples and shadows of the past symbolizing the future and now present realities (Heb. 8:1 - 5).

⁸ The Holy Ghost signifies that the way into the holiest of all was not yet made manifest, while as the first tabernacle was yet standing: ⁹ Which was a figure for the time then present, in which were offered both gifts and sacrifices, that could not make him that did the service perfect, as pertaining to the conscience; ¹⁰ Which stood only in meats and drinks, and divers washings, and carnal ordinances, imposed on them until the time of reformation.
— *KJV, Heb. 9:8–10*

God had instituted these purification and atonement rituals and their symbolic representation had served a divine purpose, which was to lead us to Christ.

Have you ever heard of a mikvah? Well to be perfectly honest with you, neither had I. I would like to encourage you to inform yourself about this word and the history and also of the use of a mikvah. I had every intention of writing and providing information about it, however, my desire is to write this book using the spiritual word of God: the Bible. I believe that it may be very beneficial for you, dear reader, to inform yourself. It is very easy start your computer and enter a search, such as: Jewish Baptism, Jewish Conversion, or Mikvah.² I have no doubt that if you will take the time to inform yourself you will be amazed. I would rather spend this time with you to talk a little more about the Amazing Grace of God. According to Jewish law, immersion in a mikvah is required for both men and women when converting to Judaism. There were three prerequisites for a proselyte coming into Judaism: circumcision, baptism, and sacrifice (Maimonides, Hilkh. Iss. Biah xiii. 5).

Chapter 3

The Birth of Christ

Therefore the Lord himself will give you a sign: The virgin will be with child and will give birth to a son, and will call him Immanuel.
— *NIV, Isa. 7:14*

[14] Since the children have flesh and blood, he too shared in their humanity so that by his death he might destroy him who holds the power of death—that is, the devil— [15] and free those who all their lives were held in slavery by their fear of death. [16] For surely it is not angels he helps, but Abraham's descendants. [17] For this reason he had to be made like his brothers in every way, in order that he might become a merciful and faithful high priest in service to God, and that he might make atonement for the sins of the people. [18] Because he himself suffered when he was tempted, he is able to help those who are being tempted.
— *NIV, Heb. 2:14-18*

[26] In the sixth month, God sent the angel Gabriel to Nazareth, a town in Galilee, [27] to a virgin pledged to be married to a man named Joseph, a descendant of David. The virgin's name was Mary. [28] The angel went to her and said, "Greetings, you who are highly favored! The Lord is with you." [29] Mary was greatly troubled at his words and wondered what kind of greeting this might be. [30] But the angel said to her, "Do not be afraid, Mary, you have found favor with God. [31] You will be with child and give birth to a son, and you are to give him the name Jesus. [32] He will

be great and will be called the Son of the Most High. The Lord God will give him the throne of his father David, [33] and he will reign over the house of Jacob forever; his kingdom will never end." [34] "How will this be," Mary asked the angel, "since I am a virgin?" [35] The angel answered, "The Holy Spirit will come upon you, and the power of the Most High will overshadow you. So the holy one to be born will be called the Son of God.

— *NIV, Luke 1:26-35*

[18] *This is how the birth of Jesus Christ came about: His mother Mary was pledged to be married to Joseph, but before they came together, she was found to be with child through the Holy Spirit.* [19] *Because Joseph her husband was a righteous man and did not want to expose her to public disgrace, he had in mind to divorce her quietly.* [20] *But after he had considered this, an angel of the Lord appeared to him in a dream and said, "Joseph son of David, do not be afraid to take Mary home as your wife, because what is conceived in her is from the Holy Spirit.* [21] *She will give birth to a son, and you are to give him the name Jesus, because he will save his people from their sins." [22] All this took place to fulfill what the Lord had said through the prophet:* [23] *"The virgin will be with child and will give birth to a son, and they will call him Immanuel" —which means, "God with us."*

— *NIV, Mat. 1:18-23*

[1] *In those days Caesar Augustus issued a decree that a census should be taken of the entire Roman world.* [2] *(This was the first census that took place while Quirinius was governor of Syria.)* [3] *And everyone went to his own town to register.* [4] *So Joseph also went up from the town of Nazareth in Galilee to Judea, to Bethlehem the town of David, because he belonged to the house and line of David.* [5] *He went there to register with Mary, who was pledged to be married to him and was expecting a child.* [6] *While they were there, the time came for the baby to be born,* [7] *and she gave birth to her firstborn, a son. She wrapped him in cloths and placed him in a manger, because there was no room for them in*

the inn. [8] And there were shepherds living out in the fields nearby, keeping watch over their flocks at night. [9] An angel of the Lord appeared to them, and the glory of the Lord shone around them, and they were terrified. [10] But the angel said to them, "Do not be afraid. I bring you good news of great joy that will be for all the people. [11] Today in the town of David a Savior has been born to you; he is Christ the Lord. [12] This will be a sign to you: You will find a baby wrapped in cloths and lying in a manger." [13] Suddenly a great company of the heavenly host appeared with the angel, praising God and saying, [14] "Glory to God in the highest, and on earth peace to men on whom his favor rests." [15] When the angels had left them and gone into heaven, the shepherds said to one another, "Let's go to Bethlehem and see this thing that has happened, which the Lord has told us about." [16] So they hurried off and found Mary and Joseph, and the baby, who was lying in the manger. [17] When they had seen him, they spread the word concerning what had been told them about this child, [18] and all who heard it were amazed at what the shepherds said to them. [19] But Mary treasured up all these things and pondered them in her heart. [20] The shepherds returned, glorifying and praising God for all the things they had heard and seen, which were just as they had been told. [21] On the eighth day, when it was time to circumcise him, he was named Jesus, the name the angel had given him before he had been conceived. [22] When the time of their purification according to the Law of Moses had been completed, Joseph and Mary took him to Jerusalem to present him to the Lord [23] (as it is written in the Law of the Lord, "Every firstborn male is to be consecrated to the Lord"), [24] and to offer a sacrifice in keeping with what is said in the Law of the Lord: "a pair of doves or two young pigeons." [25] Now there was a man in Jerusalem called Simeon, who was righteous and devout. He was waiting for the consolation of Israel, and the Holy Spirit was upon him. [26] It had been revealed to him by the Holy Spirit that he would not die before he had seen the Lord's Christ. [27] Moved by the Spirit, he went into the temple courts. When the parents brought in the child

Jesus to do for him what the custom of the Law required, [28] Simeon took him in his arms and praised God, saying: [29] "Sovereign Lord, as you have promised, you now dismiss your servant in peace. [30] For my eyes have seen your salvation, [31] which you have prepared in the sight of all people, [32] a light for revelation to the Gentiles and for glory to your people Israel." [33] The child's father and mother marveled at what was said about him. [34] Then Simeon blessed them and said to Mary, his mother: "This child is destined to cause the falling and rising of many in Israel, and to be a sign that will be spoken against, [35] so that the thoughts of many hearts will be revealed. And a sword will pierce your own soul too." [36] There was also a prophetess, Anna, the daughter of Phanuel, of the tribe of Asher. She was very old; she had lived with her husband seven years after her marriage, [37] and then was a widow until she was eighty-four. She never left the temple but worshiped night and day, fasting and praying. [38] Coming up to them at that very moment, she gave thanks to God and spoke about the child to all who were looking forward to the redemption of Jerusalem. [39] When Joseph and Mary had done everything required by the Law of the Lord, they returned to Galilee to their own town of Nazareth. [40] And the child grew and became strong; he was filled with wisdom, and the grace of God was upon him.

— NIV, Luke 2:1-40

The above verses are easy to understand; however, I do feel that further information may be helpful. I have at many times read the same verses and then all of a sudden spiritual light shines forth and I receive additional understanding. To His praise and for His glory: only

In Luke 2:21 we read, "On the eighth day, when it was time to circumcise him." Circumcision is traced back to Abraham:

[10] This is my covenant with you and your descendants after you, the covenant you are to keep: Every male among you shall be circumcised. [11] You are to undergo circumcision, and it will be the sign of the covenant between me and you.

— NIV, Gen. 17:10-11

When reading Luke 2-21-22, it is easy to understand that circumcision took place on the eighth day. What may not be easy to realize when reading these two verses is that a time span of thirty-two days are between these two verses. In Luke 2:22 we read, "When the time of their purification according to the Law of Moses had been completed, Joseph and Mary took him to Jerusalem to present him to the Lord."

Childbirth, purification and atonement:
¹ The LORD said to Moses, ² "Say to the Israelites, A woman who becomes pregnant and gives birth to a son will be ceremonially unclean for seven days, just as she is unclean during her monthly period. ³ On the eighth day the boy is to be circumcised. ⁴ Then the woman must wait thirty-three days to be purified from her bleeding. She must not touch anything sacred or go to the sanctuary until the days of her purification are over. ⁵ If she gives birth to a daughter, for two weeks the woman will be unclean, as during her period. Then she must wait sixty-six days to be purified from her bleeding. ⁶ When the days of her purification for a son or daughter are over, she is to bring to the priest at the entrance to the Tent of Meeting a year-old lamb for a burnt offering and a young pigeon or a dove for a sin offering. ⁷ He shall offer them before the LORD to make atonement for her, and then she will be ceremonially clean from her flow of blood. These are the regulations for the woman who gives birth to a boy or a girl. ⁸ If she cannot afford a lamb, she is to bring two doves or two young pigeons, one for a burnt offering and the other for a sin offering. two doves or two young pigeons, one for a burnt offering and the other for a sin offering. In this way the priest will make atonement for her, and she will be clean."
— NIV, Lev. 12:1-8

The Jewish traditions following the Laws of Moses were very complicated. A woman must not touch anything sacred or enter the sanctuary until the days of her purification were over (Lev. 12:4). A Jewish woman was forbidden to enter the tabernacle in the days of

Moses and later the Temple or a synagogue. The days of purification for a Jewish woman giving birth to a male child was forty days; only then could she bring her sacrifices to the priest. If she gave birth to a female child, a Jewish woman's days of purification would be eighty; only then was she allowed to take her sacrifices to the priest, at the entrance only. For a son or daughter: a year-old lamb for a burnt offering and a young pigeon or a dove for a sin offering. If she could not afford a lamb, then she was required to bring two doves or two young pigeons, one for a burnt offering and the other for a sin offering. In this way the priest would make atonement for her and she would be clean.

It is totally impossible to realize and become aware of these things when we only read Luke 2:21 - 22. I truly believe that there is a great difference between reading something and studying it. Unfortunately, I have not always thought this way, and I have wasted a great amount of time in the past reading right over something and not receiving any additional understanding and spiritual light. The more information or known facts we have on anything, the easier it is for any of us to understand. In my mind, information is the key which unlocks the door of understanding, bringing forth and giving knowledge. The better we understand spiritual matters, the better will be our capability of serving our precious Lord and Savior. The more we understand, the harder it also becomes for anyone to lead us away from spiritual truth. I truly believe that these verses need nothing more explained. However, I believe that it may be very helpful if we take a closer look at Luke 2:35 in the near future.

I have heard mature Christians, who I regard as more knowledgeable than myself, make the statement that the Jewish people never practiced water purification rituals before John the Baptist. It saddens my heart and I honestly have never been able to understand how these individuals could make such a statement. The point which I would like to make, is that we should realize that all Christians have areas where we need more spiritual understanding. We should always study and only then decide if what we are being told is true to God's written word.

The Lamb of God:
I have seen and I testify that this is the Son of God."
— NIV, John 1:34

When he saw Jesus passing by, he said, "Look, the Lamb of God!"
— NIV, John 1:36

Therefore, when Christ came into the world, he said: "Sacrifice and offering you did not desire, but a body you prepared for me.
— NIV, Heb. 10:5

[8] First he said, "Sacrifices and offerings, burnt offerings and sin offerings you did not desire, nor were you pleased with them" (although the law required them to be made). [9] Then he said, "Here I am, I have come to do your will." He sets aside the first to establish the second. [10] And by that will, we have been made holy through the sacrifice of the body of Jesus Christ once for all.
— NIV, Heb. 10:8-10

[18] *For you know that it was not with perishable things such as silver or gold that you were redeemed from the empty way of life handed down to you from your forefathers,* [19] *but with the precious blood of Christ, a lamb without blemish or defect.*
— NIV, 1 Peter 1:18-19

He came and preached peace to you who were far away and peace to those who were near.
— NIV, Eph. 2:17

Chapter 4

The Second Covenant

Why did Jesus preach peace between God and man? "For" or "because of" a better and New Covenant, which was not based on the Law: the Law of Moses.

[7] For if there had been nothing wrong with that first covenant, no place would have been sought for another. [8] But God found fault with the people and said: "The time is coming, declares the Lord, when I will make a new covenant with the house of Israel and with the house of Judah. [9] It will not be like the covenant I made with their forefathers when I took them by the hand to lead them out of Egypt, because they did not remain faithful to my covenant, and I turned away from them, declares the Lord.

— *NIV, Heb. 8:7-9*

[16] "This is the covenant I will make with them after that time," says the Lord. "I will put my laws in their hearts, and I will write them on their minds." [17] Then he adds: "Their sins and lawless acts I will remember no more." [18] And where these have been forgiven, there is no longer any sacrifice for sin.

— *NIV, Heb. 10:16-18*

"For I will forgive their wickedness and will remember their sins no more."

— *NIV, Heb. 8:12*

[24] *For Christ did not enter a man-made sanctuary that was only a copy of the true one; he entered heaven itself, now to appear for us in God's presence.* [25] *Nor did he enter heaven to offer himself again and again, the way the high priest enters the Most Holy Place every year with blood that is not his own.* [26] *Then Christ would have had to suffer many times since the creation of the world. But now he has appeared once for all at the end of the ages to do away with sin by the sacrifice of himself.* [27] *Just as man is destined to die once, and after that to face judgment,* [28] *so Christ was sacrificed once to take away the sins of many people; and he will appear a second time, not to bear sin, but to bring salvation to those who are waiting for him.*

— *NIV, Heb. 9:24-28*

[9] *Then he said, "Here I am, I have come to do your will." He sets aside the first to establish the second.* [10] *And by that will, we have been made holy through the sacrifice of the body of Jesus Christ once for all.* [11] *Day after day every priest stands and performs his religious duties; again and again he offers the same sacrifices, which can never take away sins.* [12] *But when this priest had offered for all time one sacrifice for sins, he sat down at the right hand of God.* [13] *Since that time he waits for his enemies to be made his footstool,* [14] *because by one sacrifice he has made perfect forever those who are being made holy.*

— *NIV, Heb. 10:9-14*

[14] *How much more, then, will the blood of Christ, who through the eternal Spirit offered himself unblemished to God, cleanse our consciences from acts that lead to death, so that we may serve the living God!* [15] *For this reason Christ is the mediator of a new covenant, that those who are called may receive the promised eternal inheritance—now that he has died as a ransom to set them free from the sins committed under the first covenant.* [16] *In the case of a will, it is necessary to prove the death of the one who made it,* [17] *because a will is in force only when somebody has died; it never takes effect while the one who made it is living.*

— *NIV, Heb. 9:14-17*

This is my blood of the covenant, which is poured out for many for the forgiveness of sins.

—NIV, Mat. 26:28

⁵⁰ And when Jesus had cried out again in a loud voice, he gave up his spirit. ⁵¹ At that moment the curtain of the temple was torn in two from top to bottom. The earth shook and the rocks split. ⁵² The tombs broke open and the bodies of many holy people who had died were raised to life. ⁵³ They came out of the tombs, and after Jesus' resurrection they went into the holy city and appeared to many people. ⁵⁴ When the centurion and those with him who were guarding Jesus saw the earthquake and all that had happened, they were terrified, and exclaimed, "Surely he was the Son of God!"

— NIV, Mat. 27:50-54

Almost two thousand years ago on a hillside outside the city walls of Jerusalem, three men on three crosses were crucified. The Hebrew name for this place is Golgotha (Mat. 27:33, Mark 15:22 and John 19:17). The Latin name is Calvary (KJV, Luke 23:33). Both names Golgotha and Calvary mean "the place of the skull."

The man nailed to the cross which stood in the middle was the Son of God. The men to His left and right were thieves and both were guilty of their crimes. The man in the middle was without sin (Heb. 4:15), yet the sins of the world were upon Him. He was the Lamb of God (John 1:29) who took our sins and nailed all of them to His cross (Col. 2:14). The man in the middle had a plaque above His head. Nailed to His cross it read: "JESUS OF NAZARETH, THE KING OF THE JEWS" (John 19:19).

Have you ever questioned why these words were written in Aramaic, Latin and Greek (John 19:20)? I believe this was done to make these words readable to everyone present. This would insure a greater amount of accusations and mocking. Logical thinking: the greater the mocking, the greater the embarrassment; the greater the embarrassment, the greater the humiliation would be for the individual to bear—just a thought! I have always thought of His crucifixion and have only given serious thought to the man in the middle. I had never given much thought to the other two crosses or to the men who were on them until very recently. However, now, when I imagine this day, I see three crosses and three men. The man in the middle is the same: the Lamb of God, my Lord and Savior. The other two men are guilty sinners. Then, I hear the words spoken by one of these men: "Aren't you the Christ? Save yourself and us!" (NIV, Luke 23:39)

A picture in my mind appears; a man being crucified for his crimes, full of sin, facing death, full of unbelief and mocking the Son of God. Sadness and sorrow fills my heart at the thought of a sinner about to die, a man of unbelief and a soul entering Hell for eternity. I hear the other man asking the man who is mocking my Lord: "Don't you fear God? We are punished justly, for we are getting what our deeds deserve. But this man has done nothing wrong" (NIV, Luke 23:40-41).

I now see in my mind this man looking at Jesus and I hear him say: "Jesus, remember me when you come into your kingdom" (NIV, Luke 23:42). A picture of this man begins to appear in my mind: a guilty man being crucified for his crimes, full of sin, facing death, a guilty man who believes the words that he read: "JESUS OF NAZARETH, THE KING OF THE JEWS," a man who has faith. I see Jesus slowly turning His head, I see Jesus looking at this believing guilty sinner who is about to die. I hear Jesus say to him, "I tell you the truth, today you will be with me in paradise" (NIV, Luke 23:43).

Then I remember the very first verse which I had learned when I was a small child: "For God so loved the world that he gave his one and only Son, that whoever believes in him shall not perish but have eternal life" (NIV, John 3:16). I think of the word "grace" and I am unable to understand His love for me and His love for you.

A sinless man full of righteousness, a man with perfect holiness, crucified for unrighteous sinners and giving His life, while we were still His enemies. In my mind I see the darkness coming in mid-day (Luke 23:44). I can hear the last words spoken by my Lord, "It is finished."(John 19:30) "Father, into your hands I commit my spirit" (NIV, Luke 23:46). I can imagine the people yelling; the veil in the temple has been torn in two (Luke 23:45). I can feel the ground shaking and I can imagine the tombs opening and the dead rising after His miraculous resurrection.

⁵⁰ And when Jesus had cried out again in a loud voice, he gave up his spirit. ⁵¹ At that moment the curtain of the temple was torn in two from top to bottom. The earth shook and the rocks split. ⁵² The tombs broke open and the bodies of many holy people who had died were raised to life. ⁵³ They came out of the tombs, and after Jesus' resurrection they went into the holy city and appeared to many people.

— NIV, Mat. 27:50-53

I also imagine the look of fear on the faces of those who were present on this historic day. The Son of God on His cross, a sign representing the sacrificial Lamb of God in the form of a man. I now see the other two men on the other crosses in a different way. I now see them as representing all of mankind. One a condemned, guilty, unsaved sinner mocking His name. This man is a sign representing all of mankind who die on the Cross of Unbelief. The other man having called on His name and been cleansed by His Blood: a guilty sinner saved by grace through faith. This man is also a sign representing all of mankind who die on the Cross of Faith, which is so easy to bear. All of mankind is on either one or the other. If you were to die today, which cross would you be on? The man in the middle, the Lamb of God, has torn the veil of separation on the Cross of Atonement.

by a new and living way opened for us through the curtain, that is, his body

— NIV, Heb. 10:20

All of mankind now has direct access to God (Eph. 3:12 and Heb. 10:19-20). Jesus is still the man in the middle, He is our Mediator and He is our High Priest (1 Tim. 2:5, Heb. 6:20). Come to Him and receive God's Amazing Grace! The old covenant has been replaced by a new covenant. Please remember my goal is to use the words of God, not the words of any man.

I would like to briefly look at a promise, which was made by God. This promise was made before the time of Moses. This promise was made to Abraham.

He took him outside and said, "Look up at the heavens and count the stars—if indeed you can count them." Then he said to him, "So shall your offspring be."

— *NIV, Gen. 15:5*

God had made a promise to Abraham and Abraham believed God's Word.

Abram believed the LORD, and he credited it to him as righteousness.

— *NIV, Gen. 15:6*

Abraham believed God's Word this is called faith. Then "he" (God) credited "it" (Abraham's faith) to him as righteousness. In other words:

Abraham's faith + God's grace = credited righteousness through faith.

The Apostle Paul was the inspired author of the Epistle to the Romans. This letter was written in Corinth, or in Cenchrea, which is a small town about six miles from Corinth. It was written to the Christians in Rome. Paul had desired to visit them for a long time. Most scholars agree that this letter was written around 56 A.D. Some major themes are: God is righteous; man is not. Salvation is only by faith in Jesus and spiritual maturity.

[4] Now when a man works, his wages are not credited to him as a gift, but as an obligation. [5] However, to the man who does not work but trusts God who justifies the wicked, his faith is credited as righteousness.

— NIV, Rom. 4:4-5

To paraphrase the above verse, wages are owed to a man for the work he has performed. Wages are an obligation, something earned. Something earned could never be thought of or given as a gift. Please remember this!

51

[20] *Therefore no one will be declared righteous in his sight by observing the law; rather, through the law we become conscious of sin.* [21] *But now a righteousness from God, apart from law, has been made known, to which the Law and the Prophets testify.* [22] *This righteousness from God comes through faith in Jesus Christ to all who believe. There is no difference,* [23] *for all have sinned and fall short of the glory of God,* [24] *and are justified freely by his grace through the redemption that came by Christ Jesus.* [25] *God presented him as a sacrifice of atonement, through faith in his blood. He did this to demonstrate his justice, because in his forbearance he had left the sins committed beforehand unpunished—* [26] *he did it to demonstrate his justice at the present time, so as to be just and the one who justifies those who have faith in Jesus.* [27] *Where, then, is boasting? It is excluded. On what principle? On that of observing the law? No, but on that of faith.* [28] *For we maintain that a man is justified by faith apart from observing the law.*

— NIV, Rom. 3:20-28

[18] *Against all hope, Abraham in hope believed and so became the father of many nations, just as it had been said to him, "So shall your offspring be."* [19] *Without weakening in his faith, he faced the fact that his body was as good as dead—since he was about a hundred years old—and that Sarah's womb was also dead.* [20] *Yet he did not waver through unbelief regarding the promise of God, but was strengthened in his faith and gave glory to God,* [21] *being fully persuaded that God had power to do what he had promised.* [22] *This is why "it was credited to him as righteousness."* [23] *The words "it was credited to him" were written not for him alone,* [24] *but also for us, to whom God will credit righteousness—for us who believe in him who raised Jesus our Lord from the dead.* [25] *He was delivered over to death for our sins and was raised to life for our justification.*

— NIV, Rom. 4:18-25

Therefore, since we have been justified through faith, we have peace with God through our Lord Jesus Christ,

— NIV, Rom. 5:1

God justifies a man when that man places his trust in Jesus (Rom. 3:22 - 24). His faith is then credited as righteousness (Rom. 4:5) by God, just like Abraham (Rom. 4:23 - 34).

[23] The words "it was credited to him" were written not for him alone, [24] but also for us, to whom God will credit righteousness— for us who believe in him who raised Jesus our Lord from the dead.

— NIV, Rom. 4:23-24

This credited righteousness is an unmerited gift from God:

For if, by the trespass of the one man, death reigned through that one man, how much more will those who receive God's abundant provision of grace and of the gift of righteousness reign in life through the one man, Jesus Christ.

— NIV, Rom. 5:17

[6] David says the same thing when he speaks of the blessedness of the man to whom God credits righteousness apart from works: [7] "Blessed are they whose transgressions are forgiven, whose sins are covered. [8] Blessed is the man whose sin the Lord will never count against him."

— NIV, Rom. 4:6-8

Justified and given the unmerited gift of righteousness through faith. By God's merciful grace plus our faith, we are credited with righteousness (Rom. 3:22-24). This unmerited gift of righteousness (Rom. 5:17) is a merciful blessing from God's complete grace. This truly is Amazing Grace.

⁸ The Scripture foresaw that God would justify the Gentiles by faith, and announced the gospel in advance to Abraham: "All nations will be blessed through you." ⁹ So those who have faith are blessed along with Abraham, the man of faith.

— NIV, Gal. 3:8-9 '

⁸ But what does it say? "The word is near you; it is in your mouth and in your heart," that is, the word of faith we are proclaiming: ⁹ That if you confess with your mouth, "Jesus is Lord," and believe in your heart that God raised him from the dead, you will be saved. ¹⁰ For it is with your heart that you believe and are justified, and it is with your mouth that you confess and are saved. ¹¹ As the Scripture says, "Anyone who trusts in him will never be put to shame."

— NIV, Rom. 10:8-11

For it is by grace you have been saved, through faith—and this not from yourselves, it is the gift of God

— NIV, Eph. 2:8

The gift of God: Salvation by Grace through Faith. I believe that the following verse in the Book of John is not only true of the Book of John, it could also be safely said to be true for the entire written word of God, the Bible.

But these are written that you may believe that Jesus is the Christ, the Son of God, and that by believing you may have life in his name.

— NIV, John 20:31

Before we visit Cornelius and Peter, I would like us to give the following term some thought. When I think of the term "the Word of God," three things light the darkness of my mind:

1. The Physical Word of God - Jesus in the flesh:

And the Word was made flesh, and dwelt among us, (and we beheld his glory, the glory as of the only begotten of the Father,) full of grace and truth.

— *KJV, John 1:14*

And he was clothed with a vesture dipped in blood: and his name is called The Word of God.

— *KJV, Rev 19:13*

2. The Inspired Written Word of God - The Bible:

And take the helmet of salvation, and the sword of the Spirit, which is the word of God

— *KJV, Eph. 6:17*

And many other signs truly did Jesus in the presence of his disciples, which are not written in this book

— *KJV, John 20:30*

3. The Spiritual Word of God - The Holy Spirit:

For the word of God is quick, and powerful, and sharper than any two-edged sword, piercing even to the dividing asunder of soul and spirit, and of the joints and marrow, and is a discerner of the thoughts and intents of the heart.

— *KJV, Hebrews 4:12*

God has provided these three elements brought to us by His Light:

I am come a light into the world, that whosoever believeth on me should not abide in darkness.

— *John 12:46*

So then faith cometh by hearing, and hearing by the word of God.

— *KJV, Rom. 10:17*

55

If spiritual truth is our goal, it is absolutely necessary that we neither add a word to Scripture nor should we ever take a word away from Scripture. The point which I am trying to stress is that we should never read anything more into Scripture nor should we ever read anything less than what is in Scripture. If we are truly responsible Christians, we must realize that our responsibility is to view Scripture as a whole. If we add a word to Scripture or if we should ever take a word away from Scripture then the Word of God has this to say:

[18] I warn everyone who hears the words of the prophecy of this book: If anyone adds anything to them, God will add to him the plagues described in this book. [19] And if anyone takes words away from this book of prophecy, God will take away from him his share in the tree of life and in the holy city, which are described in this book.

— NIV, Rev. 22:18-19

I personally also believe the above verses apply to the entire Bible and not only to the Book of Revelation. Before we trust and believe, we must hear the "message of the gospel."

Chapter 5

Peter and Cornelius

Before we visit and study the conversion of Cornelius and his household, I would like to share a favorite hymn, which comes to my mind every time I study this recorded historical conversion story.

Amazing grace! How sweet the sound
That saved a wretch like me!
I once was lost, but now am found,
Was blind, but now I see.
'Twas grace that taught my heart to fear,
And grace my fears relieved;
How precious did that grace appear
The hour I first believed!
Through many dangers, toils and snares,
I have already come;
'Tis grace hath brought me safe thus far,
And grace will lead me home.
And when we've been there ten thousand years,
Bright shining as the sun,
We'll have no less days to sing God's praise
Then when we first begun.[3]

The first detailed recorded conversion of Gentiles is found in the Book of Acts. The main characters are Cornelius and the Apostle Peter.

Cornelius has a vision:

¹ At Caesarea there was a man named Cornelius, a centurion in what was known as the Italian Regiment. ² He and all his family were devout and God-fearing; he gave generously to those in need and prayed to God regularly. ³ One day at about three in the afternoon he had a vision. He distinctly saw an angel of God, who came to him and said, "Cornelius!"⁴ Cornelius stared at him in fear. "What is it, Lord?" he asked. The angel answered, "Your prayers and gifts to the poor have come up as a memorial offering before God. ⁵ Now send men to Joppa to bring back a man named Simon who is called Peter. ⁶ He is staying with Simon the tanner, whose house is by the sea."

— NIV, Acts 10:1-6

Cornelius then sends his men to bring Peter back to him:

⁷ When the angel who spoke to him had gone, Cornelius called two of his servants and a devout soldier who was one of his attendants. ⁸ He told them everything that had happened and sent them to Joppa.

— NIV, Acts 10:7-8

Peter also receives a vision from God:

⁹ About noon the following day as they were on their journey and approaching the city, Peter went up on the roof to pray. ¹⁰ He became hungry and wanted something to eat, and while the meal was being prepared, he fell into a trance. ¹¹ He saw heaven opened and something like a large sheet being let down to earth by its four corners. ¹² It contained all kinds of four-footed animals, as well as reptiles of the earth and birds of the air. ¹³ Then a voice told him, "Get up, Peter. Kill and eat." ¹⁴ "Surely not, Lord!" Peter replied. "I have never eaten anything impure or unclean." ¹⁵ The voice spoke to him a second time, "Do not call

anything impure that God has made clean." [16] *This happened three times, and immediately the sheet was taken back to heaven.*
— *NIV, Acts 10:9-16*

Cornelius's men arrive:

[17] *While Peter was wondering about the meaning of the vision, the men sent by Cornelius found out where Simon's house was and stopped at the gate.* [18] *They called out, asking if Simon who was known as Peter was staying there.* [19] *While Peter was still thinking about the vision, the Spirit said to him, "Simon, three men are looking for you.* [20] *So get up and go downstairs. Do not hesitate to go with them, for I have sent them."* [21] *Peter went down and said to the men, "I'm the one you're looking for. Why have you come?"* [22] *The men replied, "We have come from Cornelius the centurion. He is a righteous and God-fearing man, who is respected by all the Jewish people. A holy angel told him to have you come to his house so that he could hear what you have to say."* [23] *Then Peter invited the men into the house to be his guests. The next day Peter started out with them, and some of the brothers from Joppa went along.*
— *NIV, Acts 10:17-23*

Cornelius and his household meet Peter:

[24] *The following day he arrived in Caesarea. Cornelius was expecting them and had called together his relatives and close friends.* [25] *As Peter entered the house, Cornelius met him and fell at his feet in reverence.*
— *NIV, Acts 10:24-25*

Can you imagine how Peter must have felt?

[26] *But Peter made him get up. "Stand up," he said, "I am only a man myself."* [27] *Talking with him, Peter went inside and found a*

large gathering of people. *²⁸ He said to them: "You are well aware that it is against our law for a Jew to associate with a Gentile or visit him. But God has shown me that I should not call any man impure or unclean. ²⁹ So when I was sent for, I came without raising any objection. May I ask why you sent for me?" ³⁰ Cornelius answered: "Four days ago I was in my house praying at this hour, at three in the afternoon. Suddenly a man in shining clothes stood before me ³¹ and said, 'Cornelius, God has heard your prayer and remembered your gifts to the poor. ³² Send to Joppa for Simon who is called Peter. He is a guest in the home of Simon the tanner, who lives by the sea.' ³³ So I sent for you immediately, and it was good of you to come. Now we are all here in the presence of God to listen to everything the Lord has commanded you to tell us."*

— *NIV, Acts 10:26-33*

Peter begins to preach to Cornelius and his household:

³⁴ Then Peter began to speak: "I now realize how true it is that God does not show favoritism ³⁵ but accepts men from every nation who fear him and do what is right. ³⁶ You know the message God sent to the people of Israel, telling the good news of peace through Jesus Christ, who is Lord of all. ³⁷ You know what has happened throughout Judea, beginning in Galilee after the baptism that John preached— ³⁸ how God anointed Jesus of Nazareth with the Holy Spirit and power, and how he went around doing good and healing all who were under the power of the devil, because God was with him. ³⁹ "We are witnesses of everything he did in the country of the Jews and in Jerusalem. They killed him by hanging him on a tree, ⁴⁰ but God raised him from the dead on the third day and caused him to be seen. ⁴¹ He was not seen by all the people, but by witnesses whom God had already chosen—by us who ate and drank with him after he rose from the dead. ⁴² He commanded us to preach to the people and to testify that he is the one whom God appointed as judge of the living and the dead. ⁴³ All the prophets testify about him that everyone who believes in him receives forgiveness of sins through his name. ⁴⁴ While Peter was still speaking these words, the Holy Spirit came on all who heard the message. ⁴⁵ The circumcised believers who had came with Peter were astonished that the gift of the Holy Spirit had been poured out even on the Gentiles.

— *NIV, Acts 10:34-45*

To paraphrase the last few verses, "While Peter was still speaking these words." What words? "That everyone who believes in him receives forgiveness of sins through his name." The gift of "the Holy Spirit came on all who heard the message." Remember? A gift is something that is not earned; anything earned is not and cannot be a gift! What message did they hear? "That everyone who believes in him receives forgiveness of sins through his name."

"The circumcised believers" (six Jewish Christian men) "who had come with Peter were astonished that the gift of the Holy Spirit had been poured out even on the Gentiles" (Acts 10:45).

This truly is a beautiful and wonderful recorded historical account of God's amazing unmerited complete grace and the simplicity of conversion. This includes a cleansed and purified heart, forgiveness of sins, imputed righteousness and justification, also adoption, inheritance, and the gift and seal of the Holy Spirit! God had already justified these Gentiles. God had already cleansed these Gentiles. God had already credited them with righteousness. God had already adopted them as children. God had already given them the Holy Spirit. All of these blessings given by God's grace. They were already saved, they were already born again, and they had already received the seal of the Holy Spirit!

Remission of sins, imputed righteousness, adoption, future inheritance, the gift and seal of the Holy Spirit. What more could they possibly need or want? All of these unmerited blessings were given by God's Amazing Grace. All of these blessings were received through faith by God's complete grace. All this without a single drop of water! Scripture informs us that the Holy Spirit is given to those who obey Him.

We are witnesses of these things, and so is the Holy Spirit, whom God has given to those who obey him.
— NIV, Acts 5:32

There are four separate verses in the Book of Acts which state that these Gentiles were given the gift of the Holy Spirit: Acts 10:45, 10:47, 11:17 and 15:8.

My prayers are for everyone to realize the beauty of God's complete grace in this recorded historical conversion story. You may be asking yourself: Does other Scripture support salvation before water baptism? Well, let's take a look at what is recorded by the Apostle Paul.

God presented him as a sacrifice of atonement, through faith in his blood. He did this to demonstrate his justice, because in his forbearance he had left the sins committed beforehand unpunished
— NIV, Rom. 3:25

⁶ But the righteousness that is by faith says: "Do not say in your heart, 'Who will ascend into heaven?'" (that is, to bring Christ down) ⁷ "or 'Who will descend into the deep?'" (that is, to bring Christ up from the dead). But what does it say? ⁸ "The word is near you; it is in your mouth and in your heart," that is, the word of faith we are proclaiming: ⁹ That if you confess with your mouth, "Jesus is Lord," and believe in your heart that God raised him from the dead, you will be saved. ¹⁰ For it is with your heart that you believe and are justified, and it is with your mouth that you confess and are saved.
— NIV, Rom. 10:6-10

¹⁵ I have written you quite boldly on some points, as if to remind you of them again, because of the grace God gave me ¹⁶ to be a minister of Christ Jesus to the Gentiles with the priestly duty of proclaiming the gospel of God, so that the Gentiles might become an offering acceptable to God, sanctified by the Holy Spirit.
— NIV, Rom. 15:15-16

He redeemed us in order that the blessing given to Abraham might come to the Gentiles through Christ Jesus, so that by faith we might receive the promise of the Spirit.

— NIV, Gal. 3:14

For we were all baptized by one Spirit into one body—whether Jews or Greeks, slave or free—and we were all given the one Spirit to drink.

— NIV, 1Cor. 12:13

Redemption and the gift of the Holy Spirit is by faith in the precious blood of the Lamb of God (Rom. 3:25). "And it is with your mouth that you confess and are saved" (Rom. 10:10). Complete salvation is made possible by nobody, except Jesus! We will now return to that historical day and the events of the conversion of these Gentiles.

Then Peter said:

[47] *"Can anyone keep these people from being baptized with water? They have received the Holy Spirit just as we have." * [48] *So he ordered that they be baptized in the name of Jesus Christ. Then they asked Peter to stay with them for a few days.*

— NIV, Acts 10:48

There are two parts to this verse. The first part is a question, the second part: "They have received the Holy Spirit just as we have" is a declaration made by Peter. I have three questions concerning the above verses. I truly believe that you, the reader should answer these questions.

1.   Who was Peter's order directed to?
2.   Did Peter tell them to be baptized to receive the Holy Spirit?
3.   Did Peter tell them to be baptized for the remission of sins?

Many years earlier than the conversion of these Gentiles (Acts 10: 44-45) on the Day of Pentecost, Peter had spoken the following words.

Then Peter said unto them, "Repent, and be baptized every one of you in the name of Jesus Christ for the remission of sins, and ye shall receive the gift of the Holy Ghost."

— *KJV, Acts 2:38*

Was Peter still learning and was God still teaching? I believe Peter answers this question (Acts 11:16) for us.

The Holy Spirit knew the thoughts of these men (Heb. 4:12). These Gentiles had faith in the blood of Jesus for the remission of their sins. By having faith in His precious blood for the remission of their sins, Jesus became their "sacrifice of atonement" (Rom. 3:25). They had heard the message, they had believed the message, and they had repented. That was good enough for God! God gave these men the holy spirit!

Why would God do this? To show Peter and the other six Jewish Christian men that these Gentiles had been cleansed, washed and purified by Jesus! To show Peter and his Christian Jewish brothers that these Gentile men needed nobody. Nobody, except Jesus.

This mystery is that through the gospel the Gentiles are heirs together with Israel, members together of one body, and sharers together in the promise in Christ Jesus.

— *NIV, Eph. 3:6*

For it is by grace you have been saved, through faith—and this not from yourselves, it is the gift of God

— *NIV, Eph. 2:8*

Do you remember, what was said to Mary, by Simeon?

So that the thoughts of many hearts will be revealed. And a sword will pierce your own soul too.

— *NIV, Luke 2:35.*

Our Lord, after his death and while He was still hanging on the cross, was pierced with a physical sword. When I think of that moment when a Roman sword pierced deep into His side, I am able to imagine His precious blood pouring out for the remission of our sins. What I am unable to completely imagine is the horrible pain and also the indescribable suffering my Savior endured "for" or "because" of my sins. Sorrow, disgust and guilt fills my heart, knowing that my sins were the reason for His suffering. So unworthy am I! His mother Mary was also ("too") pierced with a sword. She was pierced with a spiritual sword. Can you try to imagine the pain Mary felt? Her pain was so great and penetrated so deep that it pierced her very soul. This terrible pain did, however, have a purpose. This gracious unmerited marvelous purpose was: "so that the thoughts of many hearts will be revealed."

Think about this for a moment hopefully a very, very long moment! Everything was done for us; all we have to do is believe and repent, and at that very moment, we are given the gift and seal of the Holy Spirit! Unmerited "complete" Grace of God. May all people come to know Him and may we never cease Praising Him!

For the word of God is quick, and powerful, and sharper than any two-edged sword, piercing even to the dividing asunder of soul and spirit, and of the joints and marrow, and is a discerner of the thoughts and intents of the heart.

— KJV, Heb. 4:12

The Spirit itself beareth witness with our spirit, that we are the children of God

— KJV, Rom. 8:16

For by one Spirit are we all baptized into one body, whether we be Jews or Gentiles, whether we be bond or free; and have been all made to drink into one Spirit.

— KJV, 1Cor. 12:13

Peter's commission was to preach the gospel to the Jewish people. Here is Peter, a man filled with the Holy Spirit to the extent that he was able to raise Tabitha back to life (Acts 9:40), still being taught by God eight to tens years after the Day of Pentecost! God had already revealed this mystery to the Apostle Paul. Now, God was showing and teaching Peter, giving Peter the same spiritual understanding and the same spiritual light as Paul. God had given Peter a vision. Peter had thought that this vision was concerning the Jewish custom, prohibiting certain unclean animals to be eaten. God was still teaching, and there is no doubt that many years after the Day of Pentecost, Peter was still learning that God's amazing grace was even for the Gentiles.

This alone should be a lesson for all Christians. None of us should think that we know it all. We can always be more than we presently are. Our desire to increase our spiritual maturity should be a never-ending goal. In my opinion, all of us have areas for personal growth. Had Cornelius and these other Gentiles known the words of Amazing Grace, I could imagine in my mind them singing: *Amazing grace! How sweet the sound: That saved a wretch like me! I once was lost, but now am found, Was blind, but now I see.*

Chapter 6

"Even the Gentiles"

The Jews begin to criticize Peter:

The Apostles and the brothers throughout Judea heard that the Gentiles also had received the word of God.
— KJV, Acts 11:1

For the word of God is quick, and powerful, and sharper than any two-edged sword, piercing even to the dividing asunder of soul and spirit, and of the joints and marrow, and is a discerner of the thoughts and intents of the heart.
— KVJ, Heb. 4:12

I truly believe that the letter "w" in word in the above verses should have been capitalized by our translators. Why? Because in both verses, I believe the term "the word of God" is referring to the Holy Spirit. The Gentiles had received the Word of God, the spiritual Word of God: the Holy Spirit.

The following verses (Acts 11:2-18) are difficult for me to understand. I think about this historical day, which I like to refer to as "Peter's Day of Explaining." We have here in Peter a man who had spent three years or more with Christ. A man who had been an eyewitness to many of Christ's miracles. A man who was also an eyewitness to His resurrection, a man present on the Day of Pentecost, and a man who also performed many miracles himself, by the power of the Holy Spirit. This same man is now in Jerusalem giving a precise account to these Jewish Christians.

I ask myself: Why? Why would Peter allow anyone to question his actions when he knew they were God's instructions? This alone should help us realize that Christianity and salvation by grace through faith was in direct conflict with the Jewish tradition: obeying the Mosaic Laws, Judaism.

So when Peter went up to Jerusalem, the circumcised believers criticized him and said, "You went into the house of uncircumcised men and ate with them."

— *NIV, Acts 11:2-3*

"The circumcised believers" means the Jewish Christians. Under Jewish Law, going into the house of uncircumcised men was a big No No! We will now take a look at Peter's day of explaining:

⁴ Peter began and explained everything to them precisely as it had happened: ⁵ "I was in the city of Joppa praying, and in a trance I saw a vision. I saw something like a large sheet being let down from heaven by its four corners, and it came down to where I was. ⁶ I looked into it and saw four-footed animals of the earth, wild beasts, reptiles, and birds of the air. ⁷ Then I heard a voice telling me, 'Get up, Peter. Kill and eat.' ⁸ I replied, 'Surely not, Lord! Nothing impure or unclean has ever entered my mouth.' ⁹ "The voice spoke from heaven a second time, 'Do not call anything impure that God has made clean.' ¹⁰ This happened three times, and then it was all pulled up to heaven again. ¹¹ "Right then three men who had been sent to me from Caesarea stopped at the house where I was staying. ¹² The Spirit told me to have no hesitation about going with them. These six brothers also went with me, and we entered the man's house.

— *NIV, Acts 11:4-12*

Peter took six Jewish brothers with him to Cornelius' house without hesitation. Peter is now using these six Jewish Christian men as his witnesses. Peter may have "doubted nothing" (KJV, Acts 11:12); however, I believe that it would be safe to say that Peter was at least cautious and perhaps just a little bit nervous about going to Cornelius' house! Peter had been instructed by the Holy Spirit to go with these men, who had been sent by Cornelius. The Holy Spirit did not instruct Peter to take anyone with him to Cornelius' house. Peter was a Jew; he knew it was against Jewish Law for a Jew to have anything to do with any Gentile. Peter even went so far as to inform Cornelius of this fact (Acts 10:28).

It was common Jewish practice at this time to bring individuals with you for the purpose of having your own personal witnesses. The historical facts, which we should realize are:

1. Peter was not instructed by the Holy Spirit to take these six Jewish Christian brothers with him.
2. Peter knew that it was against Jewish law for a Jew to have anything to do with a Gentile.
3. Peter decided to take these six men with him.
4. Peter is also now using these men as his personal witnesses.

Back to Peter:

[13] He told us how he had seen an angel appear in his house and say, 'Send to Joppa for Simon who is called Peter. [14] He will bring you a message through which you and all your household will be saved.'

— NIV, Acts 11:13-14

In my opinion, these two verses are a revelation which reveals the extent of God's amazing complete grace. We are informed by these verses that an angel had told Cornelius that Peter would bring him "a message through which you and all your household will be saved." And the message was "that everyone who believes in him receives forgiveness of sins through his name" (Acts 10:43). At that very moment God gave the Holy Spirit to these Gentiles!

We are faced with a very serious question here. Why now? Why was the Holy Spirit given at this very moment? When we think of God, it is easy to realize that God is a God who is full of wisdom. It is also easy to realize that God wanted Peter and the six Jewish Christian men to know that God had purified these Gentiles. We should also realize that God also knew that the Holy Spirit would inspire the Apostle Luke to record this historical day and the events which followed. We must realize then that God also knew that this historical event would be eternally preserved for all men of all nations. When we realize that seven percent of the Book of Acts is dedicated to this historical event, we can then easily see that God wanted not only the then-present generation, but also all future generations, to realize that we need nobody. Nobody, except Jesus!

Let's get back to Peter "for" or "because" the words of God are greater and will mean more to us than the words I write.

[15] "As I began to speak, the Holy Spirit came on them as he had come on us at the beginning. [16] Then I remembered what the Lord had said: 'John baptized with water, but you will be baptized with the Holy Spirit."[4]

— NIV, Acts 11:15-16

In the above verse, the words "then I remembered" are referring to the moment when the Holy Spirit was given to the Gentiles (Acts 10:44). According to Peter, that is the moment when he remembered what the Lord had said to him: "John baptized with water, but you will be baptized with the Holy Spirit." This verse is so wonderful when we take the time to realize what is recorded here for us. Peter is acknowledging spiritual baptism. According to this statement, Peter has said that he knew "then" that these Gentiles had been baptized by the Holy Spirit. Peter also knew that these Gentiles were saved by the message he had brought to them. Peter also knew that their sins had already been forgiven. Peter also knew that they were already the children of God. This is why Peter ordered his Jewish Christian friends to baptize the Gentiles in water in the name of Jesus Christ (Acts 10:48). Both Peter and his Jewish Christian friends had to accept these Gentiles for full fellowship. Water baptism had nothing to do with their salvation; they were already saved! Peter knew that they were already the children of God! Water baptism was only an act of obedience, just as partaking of the Lord's Supper is also an act of obedience, "for" or "because" we are the children of God.

So if God gave them the same gift as he gave us, who believed in the Lord Jesus Christ, who was I to think that I could oppose God?

— *NIV, Acts 11:17*

The words "the same gift as he gave us" are referring to the Holy Spirit which had been given on the Day of Pentecost (Acts 2:2-41). Peter is now asking these Jewish Christians a question. Then Peter said: "who was I to think that I could oppose God?" Seems to me that this was an excellent question for Peter to ask these men. This question, spoken by a fisherman, is full of power. Think about it. A question so powerful that the tongues of opposition are not only brought to a halt, they were transformed to words of praise. What could they possibly do or say? Peter was only a man; he could never oppose anything which had been done by the hand of God!

When they heard this, they had no further objections and praised God, saying: "So then, God has granted even the Gentiles repentance unto life" (NIV, Acts 11:18). In others words they, the Jewish Christians did not open their mouths, except to praise God. Saying: "So then, God has granted even the Gentiles repentance unto[5] life" (Acts 11:18).

The last half of this verse is very interesting. The word "even" (NIV) or "also" (KJV) is again very revealing. If we will only take time to think about what was meant by the use of this word by these first-century Jewish Christian men. It seems to me that these Jewish individuals were both aware and also believed that they, the Jewish people, were granted; "repentance unto life." However, they are only now realizing that even the Gentiles have been given this same life by God "for" or "because" of their repentance. "Repentance unto life" means that spiritual life is granted by God "for" or "because" of their repentance. Jews repent, Gentiles repent, and both receive spiritual life from God. This is why God has commanded men everywhere to repent.

In the past God overlooked such ignorance, but now he commands all people everywhere to repent.

— NIV, Acts 17:30

This is why the Paul wrote the following verse:

For it is with your heart that you believe and are justified, and it is with your mouth that you confess and are saved.

— NIV, Rom. 10:10

Years after the conversion of Cornelius, Peter would write the following words. It is generally thought that Second Peter was written between 85 and 95 A.D., forty-five years or more after the historical day of the conversion of Cornelius and his Gentile friends.

[7] By the same word the present heavens and earth are reserved for fire, being kept for the day of judgment and destruction of ungodly men. [8] But do not forget this one thing, dear friends: With the Lord a day is like a thousand years, and a thousand years are like a day. [9] The Lord is not slow in keeping his promise, as some understand slowness. He is patient with you, not wanting anyone to perish, but everyone to come to repentance.

— NIV, 2 Pet. 3:7-9

It is easy to see from these verses that Peter is warning about a future day of judgment. It is also easy to realize Peter's increase in understanding of the spiritual light he had received throughout the previous years. Peter is also sharing with us the spiritual light, which he had received from God many years earlier, on the historical day of Cornelius's conversion. Peter tells us that God is patient with us. God does not want "anyone" to perish. Peter also informs us that God wants "everyone" to come to repentance. The word "everyone" means all people, both believers and unbelievers, both Jews and Gentiles. Anyone and everyone who repents will not perish. Can you see God's "complete" grace? This is why Jesus preached peace and reconciliation.

[16] And that he might reconcile both unto God in one body by the cross, having slain the enmity thereby: [17] And came and preached peace to you which were afar off, and to them that were nigh.

— *KJV, Eph. 2:16-17*

And that repentance and remission of sins should be preached in his name among all nations, beginning at Jerusalem.

— *KJV, Luke 24:47*

The Lord is not slow in keeping his promise, as some understand slowness. He is patient with you, not wanting anyone to perish, but everyone to come to repentance.

— *NIV, 2 Pet. 3:9*

God's Grace is so merciful that He gives spiritual life to all who believe and repent. This is why Paul wrote the following inspired verses:

For Christ did not send me to baptize, but to preach the gospel— not with words of human wisdom, lest the cross of Christ be emptied of its power. For the message of the cross is foolishness to those who are perishing, but to us who are being saved it is the power of God.

— *NIV, 1Cor. 1:17-18*

Paul also wrote the following inspired verses:

And you also were included in Christ when you heard the word of truth, the gospel of your salvation. Having believed, you were marked in him with a seal, the promised Holy Spirit.

— *NIV, Eph. 1:13*

God presented him as a sacrifice of atonement, through faith in his blood. He did this to demonstrate his justice, because in his forbearance he had left the sins committed beforehand unpunished

— *NIV, Rom. 3:25*

The Spirit himself testifies with our spirit that we are God's children.
— *NIV, Rom. 8:16*

For we were all baptized by one Spirit into one body—whether Jews or Greeks, slave or free—and we were all given the one Spirit to drink.
— *NIV, 1Cor. 12:13*

There is one body and one Spirit— just as you were called to one hope when you were called—one Lord, one faith, one baptism
— *NIV, Eph. 4:4-5*

How could God have made it any easier or plainer for us to understand? Why are so many people still unable to see the completeness of God's Amazing Grace? I honestly do not understand. My only thoughts are that Satan is a deceiver and the Master of deceitful lies. Or perhaps it is only the pride some men have of their own intellectual wisdom. The simplicity of my mind is incapable to comprehend the complexity of why.

Within this chapter was a small footnote concerning the following verse. Then I remembered what the Lord had said:

"John baptized with water, but you will be baptized with the Holy Spirit."
— *NIV, Acts 11:16*

I could never express the importance of this footnote enough. I also lack the ability to know whether or not time was taken by you to compare and study these verses. The unavailability of your Bible may have prevented you from having an opportunity to study these verses. For this reason, I have decided to provide these verses for you; however, the responsibility to study these verses belongs to nobody except you.

You and God are the only ones who know, and I believe this is the way it should be. My desire is for you to study God's written word, then decide for yourself what is true or untrue to His word. Please do not

believe that the words I write are true to the spiritual truths in the Word
of God. Study these verses and pray for the help and guidance of the
Holy Spirit to increase your understanding.

*...to be a minister of Christ Jesus to the Gentiles with the priestly
duty of proclaiming the gospel of God, so that the Gentiles might
become an offering acceptable to God, sanctified by the Holy
Spirit.*
— *NIV, Rom. 15:16*

*He redeemed us in order that the blessing given to Abraham might
come to the Gentiles through Christ Jesus, so that by faith we
might receive the promise of the Spirit.*
— *NIV, Gal. 3:14*

For we were all baptized by one Spirit into one body—whether Jews
or Greeks, slave or free—and we were all given the one Spirit to drink.
— *NIV, 1Cor. 12:13*

*21 Now it is God who makes both us and you stand firm in Christ.
He anointed us, 22 set his seal of ownership on us, and put his
Spirit in our hearts as a deposit, guaranteeing what is to come.*
— *NIV, 2Cor. 1:21-22*

*12 in order that we, who were the first to hope in Christ, might be
for the praise of his glory. 13 And you also were included in Christ
when you heard the word of truth, the gospel of your salvation.
Having believed, you were marked in him with a seal, the
promised Holy Spirit, 14 who is a deposit guaranteeing our
inheritance until the redemption of those who are God's
possession—to the praise of his glory.*
— *NIV, Eph 1:12-14*

*4 There is one body and one Spirit—just as you were called to one
hope when you were called—5 one Lord, one faith, one baptism*
— *NIV, Eph. 4:4 - 5*

Chapter 7

The First Church Council Meeting

Again, one of the surprising things about Luke's account of Peter and Cornelius is the amount of time Luke spends on it. Almost seven percent of the Book of Acts is devoted to this historical account. Most scholars agree that the first Church Council Meeting (Acts 15:4) was held in 50 A.D. In Galatians 1:18 and 2:1, Paul informs us that there was a fourteen-year span of time between his trips to Jerusalem. If we go back fourteen years from the first Church Council Meeting: (Acts 15:4) 50 A.D., Paul's first trip to Jerusalem (Acts 9:26) may have been around 36 A.D. This would place Paul's conversion around 33 A.D., three years after the crucifixion of Christ and three years after the Day of Pentecost (Acts 2:1). The conversion of Cornelius and his Gentile friends (Acts 10:43-45) was perhaps six to ten years after the Day of Pentecost. The exact accuracy of these dates is unknown. What is important is the undeniable truth that the conversion of Cornelius and his Gentile friends and family was, without a doubt, many years after the Day of Pentecost.

Years after the Day of Pentecost and years after the conversion of Cornelius and his Gentile friends, Peter would testify (Acts 15:5-11) at the first Church Council Meeting. Peter would once again explain about what God had done for Cornelius and the Gentiles on that historical day. I try to imagine in my mind being there, listening and watching history in the making. So here WE are in my mind, at the first

Church Council Meeting held in Jerusalem, almost two thousand years ago. WE will let God's written word be OUR only guide, taking US back in time to this historical recorded day. Just imagine, WE are in Jerusalem almost two thousand years ago. Barnabas, Paul, Peter and James the brother of Jesus are among some of US who are present at this church meeting. I see in my mind the Pharisees sitting. I can see on their faces, a desire to speak. WE are quietly listening and WE are filled with a desire to hear every word spoken on this historical day. In my mind, WE are looking and suddenly…

⁵ Then some of the believers who belonged to the party of the Pharisees stood up and said, "The Gentiles must be circumcised and required to obey the law of Moses." ⁶ The apostles and elders met to consider this question. ⁷ After much discussion, Peter got up and addressed them.

— NIV, Acts 15:5-7

Personal thought: Regarding the words, "After much discussion," let's be realistic. It is probably safe to say that there may have been perhaps just a little bit of arguing and even a small amount of raised voices, perhaps even a little bit of yelling going on at this church meeting. Sound familiar? Been there, done that. Me too! After all, they were dealing with a very hot topic. Oh well, I guess some things never change! I now imagine in my mind and can see Peter standing; he is beginning to speak about Cornelius and the Gentiles. I can hear Peter and I would also like you to listen…

"Brothers, you know that some time ago God made a choice among you that the Gentiles might hear from my lips the message of the gospel and believe."

— NIV, Acts 15:7

These few words spoken by Peter on this historical day are a declaration. Another personal thought: Do you remember what "message of the gospel" the Gentiles had heard and believed? That's right; "that everyone who believes in him receives forgiveness of sins through his name" (NIV, Acts 10:43). "The message of the gospel" was and is to this present day: "that everyone who believes in him receives forgiveness of sins through his name."

Listen! Peter continues to speak and WE hear Peter say:

[8] "God, who knows the heart, showed that he accepted them by giving the Holy Spirit to them, just as he did to us. [9] He made no distinction between us and them, for he purified their hearts by faith."

— NIV, Acts 15:8-9

These two verses are a mouthful. In these two short, beautiful verses, God is given the credit for five different things. Let's count them together!

1.   God knows the heart.
2.   God showed that He had accepted them.
3.   God gave them the Holy Spirit.
4.   God made no distinction between us and them.
5.   God purified their hearts by faith.

No more spiritual purification rituals (Num. 19:9) were required. They needed nobody. Nobody, except Jesus. Please do not take my understanding of these two verses of what God had done for these Gentiles to be true. Study these verses yourself. Peter is still talking. They are still listening and so should it be with me and with you.

Now then, why do you try to test God by putting on the necks of the disciples a yoke that neither we nor our fathers have been able to bear?

— NIV, Acts 15:10

This verse is greatly valuable as proof that circumcision and obeying the laws of Moses were two separate issues. You may be thinking, *No, they are the same thing.* Please don't throw this book, be patient with me, and please keep reading. Peter, who was Jewish, was speaking to the Jewish men who were present at this Church meeting. Neither Peter nor any other Jewish man would have ever thought of circumcision as a yoke which they were unable to bear. Circumcision was a seal of their covenant with God. Circumcision was a Jewish privilege and the pride of their Jewish heritage, not a yoke or burden. The laws of Moses with all of the spiritual purification rituals were the yoke! It is very important for all Christians to realize that circumcision and the Laws of Moses are not the same. WE now hear the final words spoken by Peter on this historical day.

"No! We believe it is through the grace of our Lord Jesus that we are saved, just as they are."

— NIV, Acts 15:11

There are two parts to this verse. The first part, "No!" is Peter's objection to the Pharisees and their demand that "the Gentiles must be circumcised and required to obey the law of Moses"(Acts 15:5).

The second part, "We believe it is through the grace of our Lord Jesus that we are saved, just as they are," is a declaration. I like to refer to this statement made by Peter as "The Declaration of Grace."

WE are still in Jerusalem. Then suddenly…

¹² The whole assembly became silent as they listened to Barnabas and Paul telling about the miraculous signs and wonders God had done among the Gentiles through them. ¹³ When they finished, James spoke up: "Brothers, listen to me. ¹⁴ Simon has described to us how God at first showed his concern by taking from the Gentiles a people for himself. ¹⁵ The words of the prophets are in agreement with this, as it is written: ¹⁶ 'After this I will return and rebuild David's fallen tent. Its ruins I will rebuild, and I will restore it, ¹⁷ that the remnant of men may seek the Lord, and all the Gentiles who bear my name, says the Lord, who does these things' ¹⁸ that have been known for ages. ¹⁹ "It is my judgment, therefore, that we should not make it difficult for the Gentiles who are turning to God. [20] Instead we should write to them, telling them to abstain from food polluted by idols, from sexual immorality, from the meat of strangled animals and from blood. [21] For Moses has been preached in every city from the earliest times and is read in the synagogues on every Sabbath."

— *NIV, Acts 15:12-21*

From the above words spoken by James, we can easily see that James acknowledges that Peter's testimony is in agreement with the prophecies of the Old Testament prophets. I believe that we have a very diplomatic statement here from James: "For Moses has been preached in every city from the earliest times and is read in the synagogues on every Sabbath." This statement may have been for the purpose of assurance. We are also able to realize that James seems to be in a role or position of leadership: "It is my judgment" (Acts 15:19). I am forced to ask myself, *Why James? Why not Peter or one of the original twelve?* The judgment is that "we should write to them, "telling them to abstain from": (1) "food polluted by idols," (2) "from sexual immorality," (3) "from the meat of strangled animals," and (4) "from blood."

In my opinion, we must ask ourselves the following questions concerning the above judgment and these restrictions. Do three of these four restrictions have anything at all to do with Christianity? Please notice that three of them are from the Laws of Moses, Judaism, and have nothing at all to do with Christianity. Realizing that three of these instructional restrictions have nothing at all to do with Christianity, we are then forced to face another very important and very serious question.

Was God's merciful grace and Christianity completely understood by all of these men, in 50 A.D.? Historical facts force us to only one possible conclusion!

It is easy to realize from this judgment that Christianity was struggling with traditional Judaism. Freedom from the Laws of Moses was not yet complete. The Legalism of Judaism was opposing God's Complete Grace. However, the message of the gospel: "that everyone who believes in him receives forgiveness of sins through his name" is formally accepted!

In the second chapter of this book, we were informed that obedience to the Laws of Moses required the Israelites and also the foreigners (non-Jewish people; Gentiles) to be sprinkled with "the water of cleansing" (NIV) or "water of separation" (KJV) to purify them from sin (Numbers 19:9-10). This symbolic physical water purification ritual from sin (Numbers 19:9) was instituted to teach us and to lead us to Christ. It was an example, a physical symbolic representation, of the spiritual cleansing, washing or sprinkling (1 Pet. 1:2) we receive through faith in His precious blood.

There is no requirement of circumcision at this Church Council Meeting! Obedience to the Mosaic laws was also no longer required. The sprinkling of "the water of cleansing" for sin (Numbers 19:9) was also no longer necessary. We must acknowledge that there is also no mention of water baptism! Why? Because His precious redeeming blood, which had been shed for the remission of sins, was the atonement; the ransom had been paid."The message of the gospel" is "that everyone who believes in him receives forgiveness of sins through his name." And the second reason is: one Lord, one faith, one baptism (Eph. 4:5).

There is only one baptism, which will place us into the spiritual body of Christ. Peter had also been an eyewitness to this (Acts 10:43-45). Peter knew that this one baptism, which places us into the spiritual church was not done by the hands of men. Peter knew. "Then I remembered what the Lord had said. 'John baptized with water, but you will be baptized with the Holy Spirit" (Acts 11:16).

This one baptism was and still is to this very day done by the Holy Spirit and not by the hands of men! I like to refer to this formally accepted declaration as: The Simplicity of Conversion. We need nobody, except Jesus!

For we were all baptized by one Spirit into one body—whether Jews or Gentiles, slave or free—and we were all given the one Spirit to drink.

— NIV, 1Cor. 12:13

The Spirit himself testifies with our spirit that we are God's children.
— *NIV, Rom. 8:16*

In this recorded historical account of the first Church Council Meeting, it is plain to see that the topic at this meeting was: "The Gentiles must be circumcised." However, we also must realize that this was not the only issue and was not the only demand at this meeting. The second issue was that the Gentiles must be "required to obey the law of Moses." It is not hard to understand that a declaration was also made by the Pharisees.

Then some of the believers who belonged to the party of the Pharisees stood up and said, "The Gentiles must be circumcised and required to obey the law of Moses."
— *NIV, Acts 15:5*

This is a compound declaration. The Pharisees made two separate demands. The first demand, "The Gentiles must be circumcised," is self-explanatory and requires no further discussion. However, the second demand, "and required to obey the law of Moses," requires a great amount of further information if there is a desire to fully understand what was meant and what was required "to obey the law of Moses." Circumcision and obeying the laws of Moses are two totally separate issues. Circumcision is traced back to Abraham, many centuries before the laws of Moses were given to the Jewish people.

In the first century, Jews believed that spiritual purification, justification and righteousness were only possible by those who could earn their own righteousness, by their own works or acts of righteousness. This was done only by obeying and fulfilling all of the laws of Moses. I believe most Christians may have very little information to help them to fully understand what was meant by the use of this first-century Jewish term. Most Christians only think of the Ten Commandments and are not aware of the full meaning of these words: "required to obey the laws of Moses." The Laws of Moses contain 613 written laws. I also believe that most Christians may have little or no information regarding the Oral Law, or the knowledge that the Oral Law was included and considered to be part of the written Laws of Moses.

I will attempt to provide further information in a way which will hopefully be easy to understand and not be confusing to myself or to you, the reader. However, I would like to give you a little more information about myself. Before we proceed any further, please realize that I am not trying to compare myself with Peter. I only want to remind you that Peter was a fisherman. I am writing this section at three o'clock in the morning. I believe that it may be helpful for me to have another cup of coffee before we go any further.

I work a swing shift schedule: a week of afternoons, a week of days and a week of midnights. Do you remember in the beginning of this book when I stated that I did not believe that someone had to be a scholar to understand God's plan of salvation? Well, I truly meant those words and want to share with you what I do for a living. Are you ready? I am a steel worker! Please continue to read, you have read to this point. I intend to share more with you a little later. If that information had been on the cover, you may not be reading this book right now.

The point I wish to make is that we can only receive a limited amount of information from the cover of any book. The Bible is no different from any other book. We must open the cover to understand and receive the spiritual light provided for us within its pages. Leave your Bible closed and you will never realize the beauty of the inspired written words. Spiritual maturity is only possible when efforts are made. "Do nothing; know nothing," as my dear mother always told me when I was a child. I have always held those words close to me; they have always motivated me to try to do everything to the best of my ability.

The term which Jewish people use for the Hebrew bible is "Tanakh." Tanakh is an acronym for Torah (Laws), Nevi'im (Prophets) and Ketuvim (Writings).

The "Written Law," which is known as the "Torah," contains the book Christians call the "Old Testament." Within the Torah, the laws of Moses are recorded. The books of the New Testament are not part of Jewish Scripture. Why? The reason is very simple. Orthodox Jews, which simply means, traditional Jews, have never believed that Jesus was their promised Messiah. Therefore, Orthodox Jews reject the books of the New Testament as being from God. This is why Orthodox Jews, even to this very day, believe and obey the written Laws of Moses and also the Oral Law. They believe that they are still under the first Covenant, and consider the original Covenant still binding. According to Jewish tradition, Moses is considered the greatest prophet and teacher that the Jewish people have ever known.

In the Torah, the first five books are known by their Hebrew names: Bereishith, Shemoth, Vayiqra, Bamidbar and Devarim. Together, these five books, are called "The Law." The Greek names for these same books are: Genesis, Exodus, Leviticus, Numbers and Deuteronomy. Christians know these five books as "The Pentateuch" or "The Books of Moses." Recorded within these five books of written Scripture are the 613 commandments given by God to Moses and the Jewish people at Mount Sinai, after God had led His chosen people to freedom and their deliverance from the bondage of Egyptian captivity and slavery. It is absolutely impossible to fully realize how complicated Orthodox Judaism was in the first century and how complicated Judaism remains even to this very day. The 613 commandments are only part of the requirements necessary to fulfill and "obey the law of Moses."

According to Jewish tradition, Orthodox Jews believe that God also taught Moses what they refer to as the Oral Law or Oral Torah. According to Jewish tradition, God explained to Moses how to apply and fulfill the required 613 commandments of the Written Law. Jewish tradition teaches that this Oral Torah was handed down orally from the time of Moses until the second century! This means that the Oral Torah was maintained in oral form only for fifteen- to seventeen-hundred years. The following verses spoken by Jesus are a direct reference to the Oral Torah and its traditional use among the Pharisees and the Jewish people of the first century.

They worship me in vain; their teachings are but rules taught by men. You have let go of the commands of God and are holding on to the traditions of men.

— *NIV, Mark 7:7-8*

Thus you nullify the word of God by your tradition that you have handed down. And you do many things like that.

— *NIV, Mark 7:13*

These traditions were maintained in oral form only until about the second century, when the Oral Law was written down in a document called the Mishnah. The reason for putting the Oral Law in written form was fear. The leading Jewish Rabbis of the second century were afraid that their ancient traditional Oral Law would be lost forever. Their fear stemmed from the destruction of their Temple in 70 A.D. by the Romans. They were displaced and scattered around the known world of the second century and persecuted.

It is totally impossible to provide a complete description of the complexity of fulfilling the traditional Jewish requirements for obeying the laws of Moses. I have neither the desire, time, and to be totally honest with you, the ability to completely describe these requirements. My only desire here is to hopefully help you, the reader, and also myself, to realize that there is much more to the term, "required to obey to law of Moses" than the ten commandments alone. I have received and endured many headaches while attempting to study this topic. I have no further desire to beat my sore head against the wall! I hope and pray that you have received some new information, which was easy to understand and hopefully will also be helpful to you.

For a detailed description of Hebrew traditions given in the Mishnah and the Talmud, from the point of view of Messianic Jews, please see: *A Walk of Purity (A Study of baptisms)* by Peggy Pryor. I believe that any Christian who has made the efforts to study first century church history and Jewish customs and traditions, are well aware of the historical conflicts between first century Judaism and Christianity. The Jewish custom of righteousness by works was fighting righteousness by faith. Saved by righteous acts versus saved by faith. Earned salvation versus unmerited salvation. Sacramental ritual legalism, Judaism, versus God's complete grace, Christianity.

Why could they not see that they need nobody? Nobody, except Jesus! I truly believe that you can easily inform yourself of the complexity of traditional Jewish rituals regarding spiritual purification if the desire is within you.

Chapter 8

"Unless I Wash You"

Then I remembered what the Lord had said: 'John baptized with water, but you will be baptized with the Holy Spirit.'
— *NIV, Acts 11:16*

Do you remember when we first took a closer look at this verse? This verse makes me think of other verses spoken by Jesus to Peter and recorded in the Book of John.

6 He came to Simon Peter, who said to him, "Lord, are you going to wash my feet?" 7 Jesus replied, "You do not realize now what I am doing, but later you will understand." 8 "No," said Peter, "you shall never wash my feet." Jesus answered, "Unless I wash you, you have no part with me." 9 "Then, Lord," Simon Peter replied, "not just my feet but my hands and my head as well!"
— *NIV, John 13:6-9*

When I think of the above verses, I realize that not only would Peter someday remember what the Lord had said to him concerning John's baptism and the baptism of the Holy Spirit (Acts 11:16), he would also come to realize why Jesus had washed his feet. Peter would also realize years later, what this act of foot washing had symbolized.

This was a physical act Jesus performed to symbolize what He would do in the near future on the cross/altar. Spiritual cleansing, spiritual washing, and spiritual purification were symbolized through foot washings. By washing their feet, Jesus was showing them that He

87

would shortly be purifying them on the cross with His shed blood. They did not, at this present time, understand what this act meant. However, in the near future, they would understand that they were spiritually purified and spiritually washed by His blood. Jesus would soon be the new High Priest. They were to be His Priests, however, not from the order of Aaron, which required consecration by "the water of cleansing"(Num. 8:5-7) being sprinkled on them.

⁵ The Lord said to Moses, ⁶ "Take the Levites from among the other Israelites and make them ceremonially clean. ⁷ To purify them, do this: Sprinkle the water of cleansing on them; then have them shave their whole bodies and wash their clothes, and so purify themselves."

NIV, Num. 8:5-7

The Mosaic Law also required daily ceremonial washings for purification, before Priestly service could begin (Exo. 30:19).

The atonement, His blood, would be the only atonement necessary for the remission of sins and spiritual purification. The old Mosaic laws of atonement and priestly purification and initiation would soon come to an end. They would, in the near future, understand that they were washed completely by His precious blood (Heb.10: 19-22 and Rev.1:5)

If we compare the NIV and the KJV, in verse 10, I believe that we may have a contradiction.

Jesus answered, "A person who has had a bath needs only to wash his feet; his whole body is clean. And you are clean, though not every one of you."

— NIV, John 13:10

¹⁰ Jesus saith to him, He that is washed needeth not save to wash his feet, but is clean every whit: and ye are clean, but not all.

— KJV John 13:10

The word "save" in this verse is translated from a Greek particle, which is used to make a distinction and comparison between two connecting terms. The two connecting terms that we have in this verse are: "He that is washed needeth not" and "to wash his feet." The term "He that is washed needeth not," is referring to someone who has been washed completely (Heb. 10:22) by Jesus, someone who has been washed and purified by His blood. The term "to wash his feet," is referring to the Mosaic Jewish tradition of washing the feet and hands which was a daily required water purification ritual (Exo. 30:19-21) for the Priests of the Levites. This symbolic act of foot washing occurred within the last twenty-four hours of His life and had nothing at all to do with physical cleanliness. This act of foot washing symbolized the complete spiritual washing which He would provide by His precious blood in the near future. In other words: Jesus is/was, comparing two different modes of spiritual purification. Future purification by His blood (Heb. 10:22) was being compared to the then present purification by ceremonial washings: ceremonial purification rituals by water (Exo. 30:19-21).

[7] Jesus replied, "You do not realize now what I am doing, but later you will understand." [8] "No," said Peter, "you shall never wash my feet." Jesus answered, "Unless I wash you, you have no part with me."

— *NIV, John 13:7-8*

What did Jesus mean by this term: "Unless I wash you"? Did Jesus mean *unless I wash your feet with water, Peter, you will have no part with me?* "Unless I wash you." Unless means no other way. I means The Lamb of God. Wash you means wash/cleanse you with My blood, which is pure water (Heb. 10:22). "Unless I wash you," means *Unless I, the Lamb of God, wash you with my blood, which is pure water, you will have no part with me.*

Jesus replied, "You do not realize now what I am doing, but later you will understand."

— *NIV, John 13:7*

89

Elect according to the foreknowledge of God the Father, through sanctification of the Spirit, unto obedience and sprinkling of the blood of Jesus Christ: Grace unto you, and peace, be multiplied.
— *KJV, 1 Pet. 1:2*

But ye are a chosen generation, a royal priesthood, an holy nation, a peculiar people; that ye should show forth the praises of him who hath called you out of darkness into his marvelous light.
— *KJV, 1 Pet. 2:9*

We are no different than Peter, we are also called to be Priests; we are a chosen people of a royal priesthood (1 Pet. 2:9) consecrated by the "sprinkling of the blood of Jesus," (1 Pet. 1:2) "having our hearts sprinkled from an evil conscience, and our bodies washed with pure water" (Heb. 10:22).

The required consecration ritual for Priests under the Mosaic Law by sprinkling "the water of cleansing" (Num. 8:5-7) on them was not the only water purification ritual to be annulled by Jesus going to the cross. In the second chapter of this book, we were also informed by God's written word that the Israelites were also required under the Mosaic Law to use "the water of cleansing" for the purification from sin.

"A man who is clean shall gather up the ashes of the heifer and put them in a ceremonially clean place outside the camp. They shall be kept by the Israelite community for use in the water of cleansing; it is for purification from sin."
— *NIV, Num. 19:9*

This required water purification ritual from sin, for the Israelites would also shortly be annulled by Jesus going to the cross. However, Peter and the others did not presently realize these things (John 13:7) but later Peter would understand (1 Pet. 1:2).

A new High Priest and a new covenant would "Let us draw near with a true heart in full assurance of faith, having our hearts sprinkled from an evil conscience, and our bodies washed with pure water (Heb. 10:22).

[19] Having therefore, brethren, boldness to enter into the holiest by the blood of Jesus, [20] By a new and living way, which he hath consecrated for us, through the veil, that is to say, his flesh.
— *KJV, Heb. 10:19-20*

These verses that we have just studied (John 13:6-10) bring my thoughts to other verses, which relate to our Lord and Savior and the spiritual cleansing we receive by His precious blood.

For my people have committed two evils; they have forsaken me the fountain of living waters, and hewed them out cisterns, broken cisterns, that can hold no water.
— *KJV, Jer. 2:13*

Behold, the days come, saith the LORD, that I will make a new covenant with the house of Israel, and with the house of Judah.
— *NIV, Jer. 31:31*

[16] This is the covenant that I will make with them after those days, saith the Lord, I will put my laws into their hearts, and in their minds will I write them; [17] And their sins and iniquities will I remember no more. [18] Now where remission of these is, there is no more offering for sin. [19] Having therefore, brethren, boldness to enter into the holiest by the blood of Jesus, [20] By a new and living way, which he hath consecrated for us, through the veil, that is to say, his flesh; [21] And having an high priest over the house of God; [22] Let us draw near with a true heart in full assurance of faith, having our hearts sprinkled from an evil conscience, and our bodies washed with pure water.
— *KJV, Heb. 10:16-22 (Please compare this verse to John 13:8)*

[25] I will sprinkle clean water on you, and you will be clean; I will cleanse you from all your impurities and from all your idols. [26] I will give you a new heart and put a new spirit in you; I will remove from you your heart of stone and give you a heart of flesh. [27] And

I will put my Spirit in you and move you to follow my decrees and be careful to keep my laws.

— NIV, Ezek. 36:25-27

On that day a fountain will be opened to the house of David and the inhabitants of Jerusalem, to cleanse them from sin and impurity.

— NIV, Zec. 13:1

For this is my blood of the new testament, which is shed for many for the remission of sins.

— KJV, Mat 26:28

[5] And from Jesus Christ, who is the faithful witness, and the first begotten of the dead, and the prince of the kings of the earth. Unto him that loved us, and washed us from our sins in his own blood

— KJV, Rev. 1:5

Elect according to the foreknowledge of God the Father, through sanctification of the Spirit, unto obedience and sprinkling of the blood of Jesus Christ: Grace unto you, and peace, be multiplied.

— KJV, 1 Pet. 1:2 (Please compare this verse to John 13:7)

But if we walk in the light, as he is in the light, we have fellowship one with another, and the blood of Jesus Christ his Son cleanseth us from all sin.

— KJV, 1 John 1:7

God presented him as a sacrifice of atonement, through faith in his blood. He did this to demonstrate his justice, because in his forbearance he had left the sins committed beforehand unpunished

— NIV, Rom. 3:25

"On that day," the historical day when Christ was crucified, a fountain in Jerusalem was truly opened (Zec. 13:1). A fountain of pure water has been washing our bodies from sin, sprinkling our hearts from an evil conscience and filling our hearts with assurance for almost two thousand years (Heb. 10:22). This fountain is our Lord and Savior, the Lamb of God. This pure water is His precious blood which poured from the side of our Lord when He was pierced with a physical sword. This living fountain continues to flow to this very day for you and for me. Man's only need is to place full trust in His precious blood for the remission of our sins. We truly need nobody. Nobody, except Jesus! By faith we come to "the door"(John 10:7-9). By faith in His blood, Christ becomes our Passover Lamb (Rom. 3:25 & 1Cor. 5:7). By faith, our hearts are spiritually sprinkled to cleanse us of a guilty conscience, and by faith, our bodies are spiritually washed with pure water (Heb. 10:22 & 1 Pet. 1:2). By faith, we have confidence to enter the Most Holy Place by the blood of Jesus (Heb. 10:19). By faith, we approach the throne of grace with confidence, so that we may receive mercy and find grace (Heb. 4:16). Only by faith do we repent, and only by repentance are we forgiven and converted (Acts 3:19 & Acts 11:18).

The Lord is not slow in keeping his promise, as some understand slowness. He is patient with you, not wanting anyone to perish, but everyone to come to repentance.
— NIV, 2 Pet. 3:9

[8] But what does it say? "The word is near you; it is in your mouth and in your heart," that is, the word of faith we are proclaiming: [9] That if you confess with your mouth, "Jesus is Lord," and believe in your heart that God raised him from the dead, you will be saved. [10] For it is with your heart that you believe and are justified, and it is with your mouth that you confess and are saved.
— NIV, Rom. 10:8-10

[12] When he had finished washing their feet, he put on his clothes and returned to his place. "Do you understand what I have done for you?" he asked them. [13] "You call me 'Teacher' and 'Lord,'

and rightly so, for that is what I am. [14] Now that I, your Lord and Teacher, have washed your feet, you also should wash one another's feet. [15] I have set you an example that you should do as I have done for you. [16] I tell you the truth, no servant is greater than his master, nor is a messenger greater than the one who sent him. [17] Now that you know these things, you will be blessed if you do them.

— NIV, John 13:12-17

From the above verses, we are also able to realize that Jesus was teaching His disciples to be humble and to serve one another.

Chapter 9

Born Again

Years after the first Church Council of 50 A.D., Peter would write the following verses in his First Epistle, once again illustrating his increase of spiritual understanding and his knowledge of God's Amazing Grace. Scholars generally agree that First Peter was written around 63 or 64 A.D. Do you remember the term: "the word of God"? The Spiritual Word of God: The Holy Spirit

[23] Being born again, not of corruptible seed, but of incorruptible, by the word of God, which liveth and abideth for ever. [24] For all flesh is as grass, and all the glory of man as the flower of grass. The grass withereth, and the flower thereof falleth away.
— KJV, 1 Peter 1:23-24

Let's take a close look at the elements of these two verses.
1.   Natural birth-corruptible seed
2.   All flesh is like grass
3.   Glory of man-like flower of grass
4.   Born again of incorruptible seed, by the word of God.
I would like to share with you my present understanding of these verses.

Natural birth, we are all descendants of the first Adam: corruptible seed. By natural birth, we are all born of corruptible seed, born of the flesh, living to serve the desires of the flesh. Self-serving, self-satisfying, self-centered and full of sin is our natural nature; flesh is flesh, full of sin. Self-satisfying is our natural state of mind and desire.

95

All flesh is like grass. Both physically grow and their strength and beauty withers away and they both die. The flower of grass: its glory falls away and remains no more. Likewise, the flower of man: his youth, his strength, his vain glory, his works of righteousness and his earthly treasures all of his vain glory also fall away and remains no more just like the glory of grass. The glory of man is no different from the glory of grass: in the end; neither mean anything.

Christ is the last or second Adam, the incorruptible seed, the fullness of holy righteousness, without sin. "Being born again" of incorruptible seed, "by the word of God which liveth and abideth for ever." Being born again refers to spiritual birth or rebirth. The second Adam is Christ, from the seed of Abraham, the father of us all (1 Cor. 15:45). Christ is the incorruptible seed.

By faith we are led to confession and repentance. We are justified by faith, imputed righteousness and adoption. We are sealed with or by the spiritual Word of God: the Holy Spirit, which liveth and abideth for ever. Spiritual death, spiritual crucifixion, by faith and through His power. Through spiritual rebirth, we are now living and walking: by the Spirit, by His grace and through faith. Born again, by the word of God (the Holy Spirit), which liveth and abideth for ever.

This is exactly what God had shown Peter when Cornelius and the other Gentiles which were with him when they were spiritually baptized by the Holy Spirit into the body of Christ, His spiritual church, before they were baptized in water! Well, here it is, I will finally say it. To insure that there is no misinterpretation, what I am saying is this: "I believe that a person is saved before they are baptized in water.' "

One Lord, one faith, one baptism.

— KJV, Eph. 4:5

The Spirit itself beareth witness with our spirit, that we are the children of God

— KJV, Rom. 8:16

For with the heart man believeth unto righteousness; and with the mouth confession is made unto salvation.

— KJV, Rom. 10:10

"Amazing Grace, how sweet the sound, to save a wretch like me…." Our spiritual birth being "born again" is dependent on God's amazing unmerited grace and repenting faith. Think about the word faith. When I do, I ask myself the following question. Is it possible to really have faith and not repent? No. God's Grace, plus Faith. True faith will bring us to confession and repentance. "With the mouth, confession is made unto salvation" (Rom. 10:10) then by God's merciful grace we receive the gift and seal of the Holy Spirit. This was all made possible by nobody, except Jesus.

It may be helpful to look at other verses, which contain the phrase "born again."

³ Jesus answered and said unto him, Verily, verily, I say unto thee, Except a man be born again, he cannot see the kingdom of God. ⁴ Nicodemus saith unto him, How can a man be born when he is old? can he enter the second time into his mother's womb, and be born? ⁵ Jesus answered, Verily, verily, I say unto thee, Except a man be born of water and of the Spirit, he cannot enter into the kingdom of God. ⁶ That which is born of the flesh is flesh; and that which is born of the Spirit is spirit. ⁷ Marvel not that I said unto thee, Ye must be born again. ⁸ The wind bloweth where it listeth, and thou hearest the sound thereof, but canst not tell whence it cometh, and whither it goeth: so is every one that is born of the Spirit.

— KJV, John 3:3-8

In verse three, Jesus informs Nicodemus: "Except a man be born again, he cannot see the kingdom of God." Nicodemus then asks, "can he enter a second time into his mother's womb and be born?" In verse five, Jesus tells him that "Except a man be born of water and of the Spirit, he cannot enter into the kingdom of God." My present understanding of these verses is that in verse six, Jesus is aware that Nicodemus still does not understand the words spoken to him in verse five ("born of water" and "of the Spirit"). It seems to me that in verse six, Jesus clarifies His previous statement. "Born of the flesh" is referring to "born of water" and "born of the Spirit" is referring to "of the Spirit."

97

Before our natural birth, a sac surrounds an unborn child which is full of fluid or water. Prior to physical birth, this sac ruptures and the fluid springs forth and the birth of the child shortly follows. "Born of water" is our natural physical birth; flesh is flesh. It is necessary to be "born of water" for the possibility of a second birth. "Born of the Spirit" or "born again" is a spiritual birth. Our second birth is a spiritual birth by the spiritual word of God, the Holy Spirit, by the incorruptible seed: Jesus Christ.

Being born again, not of corruptible seed, but of incorruptible, by the word of God, which liveth and abideth for ever.
— *KJV, 1 Pet. 1:23*

The indwelling of the Holy Spirit signifies our faith-repentance and our spiritual rebirth. We have decided to change our sinful ways of the flesh; we have repented and no longer have a desire to fulfill the lust of the flesh. We have been reborn. Our old nature has been spiritually crucified with Christ and we are new creatures. Spiritual crucifixion of the old man and spiritual rebirth are only made possible by hearing and believing the physical inspired written word of God, the Bible. Faith leads to repentance, spiritual rebirth, spiritual life and hopefully a lifelong journey of continuous spiritual growth and maturity!

[8] But what saith it? The word is nigh thee, even in thy mouth, and in thy heart: that is, the word of faith, which we preach; [9] That if thou shalt confess with thy mouth the Lord Jesus, and shalt believe in thine heart that God hath raised him from the dead, thou shalt be saved. [10] For with the heart man believeth unto righteousness; and with the mouth confession is made unto salvation.
— *KJV, Rom. 10:8-10*

[6] For to be carnally minded is death; but to be spiritually minded is life and peace. [7] Because the carnal mind is enmity against God: for it is not subject to the law of God, neither indeed can be. [8] So then they that are in the flesh cannot please God. [9] But ye are not in the flesh, but in the Spirit, if so be that the Spirit of God

dwell in you. Now if any man have not the Spirit of Christ, he is none of his. [10] And if Christ be in you, the body is dead because of sin; but the Spirit is life because of righteousness. [11] But if the Spirit of him that raised up Jesus from the dead dwell in you, he that raised up Christ from the dead shall also quicken your mortal bodies by his Spirit that dwelleth in you. [12] Therefore, brethren, we are debtors, not to the flesh, to live after the flesh. [13] For if ye live after the flesh, ye shall die: but if ye through the Spirit do mortify the deeds of the body, ye shall live. [14] For as many as are led by the Spirit of God, they are the sons of God. [15] For ye have not received the spirit of bondage again to fear; but ye have received the Spirit of adoption, whereby we cry, Abba, Father. [16] The Spirit itself beareth witness with our spirit, that we are the children of God

— *KJV, Rom. 8:6-16*

For the word of God is quick, and powerful, and sharper than any two-edged sword, piercing even to the dividing asunder of soul and spirit, and of the joints and marrow, and is a discerner of the thoughts and intents of the heart.

— *KJV, Heb. 4:12*

As we study the written word of God, the Bible, it is absolutely necessary that we pray and ask for the help and guidance of the Holy Spirit. It is also necessary that we remember that Jesus taught many things in parables and stated His reason for doing so. It is also necessary not only to realize but also to remind ourselves that many times words are written as symbols or written symbolically. Every time we read the word "baptism" or "baptized" in the New Testament, we should also remind ourselves that these two words do not always refer to a baptism in or with water. A very good example of this is found in the following verses.

And were all baptized unto Moses in the cloud and in the sea

— *KJV, 1Cor. 10:2*

99

For by one Spirit are we all baptized into one body, whether we be Jews or Gentiles, whether we be bond or free; and have been all made to drink into one Spirit.

— *KJV, 1Cor. 12:13*

I would also like us to take a close look at two more verses written by Peter. I have spent many hours in prayer and many more hours studying these verses. May I please again remind you that this is only my present understanding of these verses?

[20] Which sometime were disobedient, when once the longsuffering of God waited in the days of Noah, while the ark was a preparing, wherein few, that is, eight souls were saved by water. [21] The like figure whereunto even baptism doth also now save us (not the putting away of the filth of the flesh, but the answer of a good conscience toward God,) by the resurrection of Jesus Christ

— *KJV, 1 Peter 3:20-21*

My present understanding of the above verses is as follows. The physical water did not save Noah and his family. The physical water was the result of forty days and forty nights of rain. Water was the physical element God used to destroy the disobedient sinners of Noah's time. The ark physically saved Noah and his family; the physical water did not save them. Water was the element which brought destruction to sinners.

The physical existence of the ark was only possible by God's merciful grace. God had told Noah that He would destroy all flesh. Noah was instructed by God to build the ark. The physical existence of the ark was also dependent on Noah's faith. Revelation by the Word of God, the Holy Spirit in itself, would not have delivered or saved Noah and his family. Faith in God's Word was as necessary as the revelation given by God's Word. The ark was a physical spiritual gift, given by God's grace and dependent on Noah's faith, just as our Lord and our salvation are spiritual gifts given by God's grace and received through or by faith.

During the time the ark was being built and also at the time of Noah's deliverance, the ark was a physical sign, which signified God's gift and Noah's faith for all to see. The ark was the last thing seen by the people before they perished. Just as circumcision was a spiritual physical sign, which signified Abraham's faith, so was the ark. Just as the living Word, Jesus Christ was a physical figure while He lived on earth. Just as the indwelling of the Holy Spirit signifies our faith in the Lord's death, resurrection, and ascension. This spiritual gift is the fulfillment of His promise. Given by His grace and received only through faith and repentance.

In 1 Peter 3:20 we read: "eight souls were saved by water." However in Hebrews 11:7 we read: "By faith Noah, being warned of God of things not seen as yet, moved with fear, prepared an ark to the saving of his house; by the which he condemned the world, and became heir of the righteousness which is by faith."

[37] In the last day, that great day of the feast, Jesus stood and cried, saying, If any man thirst, let him come unto me, and drink. [38] He that believeth on me, as the scripture hath said, out of his belly shall flow rivers of living water. [39] (But this spake he of the Spirit, which they that believe on him should receive: for the Holy Ghost was not yet given; because that Jesus was not yet glorified.)
— KJV, John 7: 37-39

In these verses, John informs us that the word "water" was used by Jesus symbolically for "the Holy Spirit." The following verses are only a few of many which use the word "water" symbolically for the Holy Spirit: John 4:10, John 4:14.

In Hebrews 11:7 (KJV) we read, "prepared an ark to the saving of his house." Noah's house was not saved. The word "house" is used symbolically, to represent Noah and his family: eight souls in all. Symbolic use of words is common throughout Scripture. We also read here that Noah's "house" or his family was saved by the ark. The ark physically represented the Holy Spirit and Noah's faith. The ark was a spiritual gift given by God's grace and only became a reality by or because of Noah's faith and his obedience.

In 1 Peter 3:21, Peter is comparing a "baptism" to something in the previous verse. He tells us that this baptism saves us from a bad conscience towards God. Peter also informs us what this baptism does not do. According to Peter, this baptism is "not the putting away of the filth of the flesh." The term "the filth of the flesh" is a symbolic term for the sins of the flesh! Peter is comparing this baptism to the ark. The ark represented Noah's faith and the Holy Spirit. This baptism, which Peter is referring to, assures us of a good conscience towards God. How is this possible? At the end of this verse, Peter informs us, "by the resurrection of Jesus Christ" (1 Pet. 3:21). His resurrection was dependent on His death on the cross. His ascension was dependent on His miraculous resurrection. The Holy Spirit, which Jesus had promised to send, assures us of a good conscience towards God (Rom. 8:16).

In whom we have redemption through his blood, the forgiveness of sins, according to the riches of his grace.

— KJV, Eph. 1:7

[13] In whom ye also trusted, after that ye heard the word of truth, the gospel of your salvation: in whom also after that ye believed, ye were sealed with that holy Spirit of promise, [14] Which is the earnest of our inheritance until the redemption of the purchased possession, unto the praise of his glory.

— KJV, Eph. 1:13-14

[15] For ye have not received the spirit of bondage again to fear; but ye have received the Spirit of adoption, whereby we cry, Abba, Father. [16] The Spirit itself beareth witness with our spirit, that we are the children of God.

— KJV, Rom. 8:15-16

This "baptism" which Peter is referring to and comparing to the ark as a "like figure" or sign, in my opinion, is not a water baptism. It is a spiritual baptism. We receive the Holy Spirit and are sealed with the Holy Spirit the moment we repent and trust Jesus as our Lord. The indwelling of the Holy Spirit bears witness with our spirit (Rom. 8-16).

This assures us that we are the children of God. This in turn provides us with a "good conscience towards God." How? "By the resurrection of Jesus Christ." His resurrection was necessary and also enabled Him to fulfill His promise of sending the Holy Spirit after His Ascension.

[19] *Therefore, brothers, since we have confidence to enter the Most Holy Place by the blood of Jesus,* [20] *by a new and living way opened for us through the curtain, that is, his body,* [21] *and since we have a great priest over the house of God,* [22] *let us draw near to God with a sincere heart in full assurance of faith, having our hearts sprinkled to cleanse us from a guilty conscience and having our bodies washed with pure water.*

— NIV, Heb. 10:19-22

[4] *There is one body, and one Spirit, even as ye are called in one hope of your calling;* [5] *One Lord, one faith, one baptism.*

— KJV, Eph. 4:4-5

...know that a man is not justified by observing the law, but by faith in Jesus Christ. So we, too, have put our faith in Christ Jesus that we may be justified by faith in Christ and not by observing the law, because by observing the law no one will be justified.

— NIV, Gal. 2:16

No, a man is a Jew if he is one inwardly; and circumcision is circumcision of the heart, by the Spirit, not by the written code. Such a man's praise is not from men, but from God.

— NIV, Rom. 2:29

For the word of God is living and active. Sharper than any double-edged sword, it penetrates even to dividing soul and spirit, joints and marrow; it judges the thoughts and attitudes of the heart.

— NIV, Heb. 4:12

In whom also ye are circumcised with the circumcision made without hands, in putting off the body of the sins of the flesh by the circumcision of Christ

— KJV, Col. 2:11

For as the body is one, and hath many members, and all the members of that one body, being many, are one body: so also is Christ. 13. For by one Spirit are we all baptized into one body, whether we be Jews or Gentiles, whether we be bond or free; and have been all made to drink into one Spirit. 14. For the body is not one member, but many.

— KJV, 1Cor. 12:12-14

Individuals who believe in baptismal regeneration attempt to use this verse (1 Pet. 3:21) to support their theology. If attempts are made to closely study this verse, then it is very easy to realize that this verse should never be used by anyone attempting to prove the theology of baptismal regeneration, even when agreement has been made that Peter is referring to a water baptism in this verse and not a spiritual baptism. The reason is that Peter informs us in this verse what this baptism does and also what this baptism does not do.

The like figure whereunto even baptism doth also now save us (not the putting away of the filth of the flesh, but the answer of a good conscience toward[6] God,) by the resurrection of Jesus Christ

— KJV, 1 Pet. 3:21

We must realize that First Peter was written around 63 A.D.; thirty years or more after the events of Acts 2:38! This baptism, according to Peter, does not put away, take away or wash away the filth of the flesh. The term "the filth of the flesh" is a symbolic term for the sins of the flesh! (Psalms 53:3 & Isaiah 64:6 (KJV)." There is no remission of sins in this baptism! This baptism is "the answer of a good conscience toward God." This baptism saves us from a bad conscience towards God.

Chapter 10

Spiritual Circumcision

When we are discussing spiritual issues we must realize that there are physical and spiritual things which we must compare with each other. This comparison is only possible when efforts have been made to understand these spiritual elements. Some comparative examples are:

1. Physical Church / Spiritual Church
2. Physical Birth / Spiritual Birth
3. Physical Body / Spiritual Body
4. Physical Baptism / Spiritual Baptism
5. Physical Death / Spiritual Death
6. Physical Seal / Spiritual Seal
7. Physical Circumcision / Spiritual Circumcision
8. Physical Sword / Spiritual Sword

We are informed by God's written word that there are two different circumcisions. One is physical and one is spiritual. I would like to share with you my present understanding of spiritual circumcision:

Circumcision of the Heart

²⁸ A man is not a Jew if he is only one outwardly, nor is circumcision merely outward and physical. ²⁹ No, a man is a Jew if he is one inwardly; and circumcision is circumcision of the heart, by the Spirit, not by the written code. Such a man's praise is not from men, but from God.

— NIV, Rom. 2:28-29

For the word of God is living and active. Sharper than any double-edged sword, it penetrates even to dividing soul and spirit, joints and marrow; it judges the thoughts and attitudes of the heart.

— *NIV, Heb. 4:12*

In him you were also circumcised, in the putting off of the sinful nature, not with a circumcision done by the hands of men but with the circumcision done by Christ.

— *NIV, Col. 2:11*

"Putting off of the sinful nature." When does this happen? Before or after repentance? In Hebrews 4:12, the term "the word of God" is referring to the Holy Spirit. For this reason, I believe that our translators should have capitalized the letter w in "word," in this verse. I would like us to remember once again that in Hebrews 4:12 we are informed that the Word of God "judges the thoughts and attitudes of the heart." What made this possible?

so that the thoughts of many hearts will be revealed. And a sword will pierce your own soul too.

— *NIV, Luke 2:35*

These words were spoken to Mary by Simeon. The pain of seeing her Son crucified would be so great and it would penetrate so deep, that this pain would spiritually pierce her very soul. I believe that this pain, as great as it was, served a marvelous purpose, it would reveal "the thoughts of many hearts."

My present understanding is that Mary was pierced with a spiritual sword and this would enable the thoughts of many hearts to be revealed to the Holy Spirit. This would then enable repentant believers to be given the gift of the indwelling of the Holy Spirit. This then would insure that God's laws or His commandments would then be written in our hearts.

[31] "The time is coming," declares the LORD, "when I will make a new covenant with the house of Israel and with the house of Judah. [32] It will not be like the covenant I made with their forefathers when I took them by the hand to lead them out of Egypt, because they broke my covenant, though I was a husband to them, " declares the LORD. [33] "This is the covenant I will make with the house of Israel after that time," declares the LORD. "I will put my law in their minds and write it on their hearts. I will be their God, and they will be my people.

— NIV, Jer. 31:31-33

[26] I will give you a new heart and put a new spirit in you; I will remove from you your heart of stone and give you a heart of flesh. [27] And I will put my Spirit in you and move you to follow my decrees and be careful to keep my laws.

— NIV, Eze.36:26-27:

Take the helmet of salvation and the sword of the Spirit, which is the word of God.

— NIV, Eph. 6:17

In the above verse, we again read the term "the word of God." We are also informed in this verse that "the word of God" is "the sword of the Spirit." This sword is not a physical sword, it is a spiritual sword. In this verse, the term "the word of God" is referring to the inspired written record and testimony of Jesus Christ, the written word of God, the Bible. The written "word of God" is the spiritual sword of the Holy Spirit.

This spiritual sword (Eph. 6:17) preaching Christ crucified, is so powerful that when it is preached (1Cor. 1:18) and heard (faith comes by hearing; Romans 10:17) it is able to pierce the hardness and sin of unbelief. The unbeliever's heart of stone is spiritually pierced, spiritually cut, spiritually pricked by this powerful spiritual sword. This piercing, cutting or pricking of the heart by His spiritual sword is the circumcision of the heart by the Holy Spirit. This is why witnessing is so important. A heart of stone is spiritually removed and a new heart of flesh is spiritually given (Ezek. 36:26). After a heart has been spiritually circumcised, only then is conviction and guilt possible! By hearing the sword of the Spirit (Eph. 6:17), a heart of stone is removed (Ezekial 36:26-27) and a new heart of flesh is the gift of "the circumcision of the heart"(Rom. 2:29) "done by the Spirit."

Is guilt possible from a heart of stone? Can the Holy Spirit convict an uncircumcised heart of stone? Can a heart of stone be converted? As it is written:

All of us have become like one who is unclean, and all our righteous acts are like filthy rags; we all shrivel up like a leaf, and like the wind our sins sweep us away.
— NIV, Isa. 64:6

[10] As it is written, There is none righteous, no, not one: [11] There is none that understandeth, there is none that seeketh after God. [12] They are all gone out of the way, they are together become unprofitable; there is none that doeth good, no, not one.
— KJV, Rom. 3:10-12

So then faith cometh by hearing, and hearing by the word of God.
— KJV, Rom. 10:17

[8] When he comes, he will convict the world of guilt in regard to sin and righteousness and judgment: [9] in regard to sin, because men do not believe in me
— NIV, John 16:8-9

Guilt brings conviction, conviction gives birth to faith, and faith is necessary for repentance! A heart of stone has no possibility of conviction.

The Lord is not slow in keeping his promise, as some understand slowness. He is patient with you, not wanting anyone to perish, but everyone to come to repentance.
— NIV, 2 Pet. 3: 9

⁹ That if you confess with your mouth, "Jesus is Lord," and believe in your heart that God raised him from the dead, you will be saved. ¹⁰ For it is with your heart that you believe and are justified, and it is with your mouth that you confess and are saved.

— *NIV, Rom. 10:9-10*

For the word of God is living and active. Sharper than any double-edged sword, it penetrates even to dividing soul and spirit, joints and marrow; it judges the thoughts and attitudes of the heart.

— *NIV, Heb. 4:12*

¹³ And you also were included in Christ when you heard the word of truth, the gospel of your salvation. Having believed, you were marked in him with a seal, the promised Holy Spirit, ¹⁴ who is a deposit guaranteeing our inheritance until the redemption of those who are God's possession—to the praise of his glory.

— *NIV, Eph. 1:13-14*

¹⁵ For you did not receive a spirit that makes you a slave again to fear, but you received the Spirit of sonship. And by him we cry, "Abba, Father." ¹⁶ The Spirit himself testifies with our spirit that we are God's children.

— *NIV, Rom. 8:15-16*

The Holy Spirit is the spiritual seal, which represents: (1) the spiritual circumcision of the heart (2) our faith and act of repentance (3) our spiritual birth (4) our adoption and (5) our future inheritance. I presently believe that circumcision of the heart is not the same as the indwelling of the Holy Spirit. Circumcision of the heart enables conviction and occurs before our act of personal repentance. When we sincerely repent, the Holy Spirit has the ability and the power to know a true and sincere heart of repentance. The Holy Spirit judges the thoughts and attitudes of the heart (Heb. 4:12) and is a discerner of the thoughts and intents of the heart, when we repent.

The indwelling of the Holy Spirit occurs only after an act of sincere personal repentance (Acts 10:45 & Acts 11:18). The gift of the Spirit then enables and insures that the laws or commandments of God will then be written in our heart by the indwelling and power of the Holy Spirit. The Holy Spirit is then able to guide and teach newborn Christians to spiritual understanding and true spiritual knowledge. The spiritual light, which we receive from the Holy Spirit, enables us to grow and mature spiritually: Only if we yield to and walk by the Spirit and are not lead by the flesh!

This is exactly what happened in the Book of Acts concerning Cornelius and his Gentile friends (Acts 10:43-45). Pieces of the whole conforming to the whole! We need nobody. Nobody, except Jesus! Had Cornelius and his friends known the sweet words of Amazing Grace, I could once again imagine the following words being sung by them: *Amazing Grace how sweet the sound, to save a like wretch me...* You may be asking yourself: *Does Scripture support this understanding of the heart of man being spiritually circumcised by the spiritual sword of the Holy Spirit before man has faith?* I will again let you answer this question; however, before you do, please read the following verse first.

Now when they heard this, they were pricked in their heart, and said unto Peter and to the rest of the apostles, Men and brethren, what shall we do?

— *KJV, Acts 2:37*

Just in case you answered "no" to the previous question, may we please study some verses written by the Apostle Paul? I really appreciate these verses, my prayers are that you will also pray and study them and grow and mature spiritually when you have done so. My prayers are also that all of God's children will come to realize the importance of prayer when studying the written word of God.

THE WISDOM OF GOD

[11] My brothers, some from Chloe's household have informed me that there are quarrels among you [12] What I mean is this: One of you says, "I follow Paul"; another, "I follow Apollos"; another, "I follow Cephas "; still another, "I follow Christ." [13] Is Christ divided? Was Paul crucified for you? Were you baptized into the name of Paul? [14] I am thankful that I did not baptize any of you except Crispus and Gaius [15] so no one can say that you were baptized into my name. [16] (Yes, I also baptized the household of Stephanas; beyond that, I don't remember if I baptized anyone else.) [17] For Christ did not send me to baptize, but to preach the gospel—not with words of human wisdom, lest the cross of Christ be emptied of its power. [18] For the message of the cross is foolishness to those who are perishing, but to us who are being saved it is the power of God. [19] For it is written: "I will destroy the wisdom of the wise; the intelligence of the intelligent I will frustrate." [20] Where is the wise man? Where is the scholar? Where is the philosopher of this age? Has not God made foolish the wisdom of the world? [21] For since in the wisdom of God the world through its wisdom did not know him, God was pleased through the foolishness of what was preached to save those who believe. [22] Jews demand miraculous signs and Greeks look for wisdom, [23] but we preach Christ crucified: a stumbling block to Jews and foolishness to Gentiles, [24] but to those whom God has called, both Jews and Greeks, Christ the power of God and the wisdom of God. [25] For the foolishness of God is wiser than man's wisdom, and the weakness of God is stronger than man's strength. [26] Brothers, think of what you were when you were called. Not many of you were wise by human standards; not many were influential; not many were of noble birth. [27] But God chose the foolish things of the world to shame the wise; God chose the weak things of the world to shame the strong. [28] He chose the lowly things of this world and the despised things—and the things that are not—to nullify the things that are, [29] so that no one may boast before him.

³⁰ It is because of him that you are in Christ Jesus, who has become for us wisdom from God—that is, our righteousness, holiness and redemption.

— NIV 1Cor. 1:11-30

What is Paul saying in these verses? Some of the Corinthian Christians were walking around saying to one another; "I am of Paul"(KJV), meaning that Paul had baptized them, another one was saying, "I am of Apollos"(KJV), meaning I was baptized by Apollos. Paul informs them and us that he is thankful to God that he had only baptized a few of them. Paul also informs the Corinthians and us in the seventeenth verse that Christ sent him "not to baptize, but to preach the gospel"(KJV).

We are forced to ask ourselves a very serious question here. If baptism is a requirement for salvation, then why did Christ send Paul to preach the gospel and not to baptize? What does Paul mean by this? "For Christ did not send me to baptize, but to preach the gospel—not with words of human wisdom, lest the cross of Christ be emptied of its power."

Why was Paul sent "not to baptize"? In this same verse, we are told the reason why Paul was sent not to baptize. The purpose was to preserve the power of the cross of Christ: "lest the cross of Christ be emptied of its power." There is power in this spiritual sword, preaching Christ crucified. Power so mighty and so full of God's strength that the spiritual strongholds of Satan are destroyed by preaching Christ crucified. The spiritual darkness of man, man's lack of spiritual understanding, man's hardened heart of stone, and man's sin of unbelief, can be pierced or cut by this powerful and mighty spiritual sword. In my opinion, there is no doubt that Paul has made a distinction between baptism and preaching the gospel. Paul informs us that the "message of the cross" is the power of God. God's power can save those who believe the "message of the cross."

By the wisdom of men, the world did not know God. The Jews required a sign and the Greeks seek wisdom. The preaching of Christ crucified would be foolishness to the Greeks and a stumbling block for

112

the Jews. The Jews believed in the Law, righteousness by works, self-righteousness, justified by works, saved by works. Paul informs us in verse 18 that the "message of the cross is foolishness to those who are perishing," but to those "who are being saved it is the power of God."

Paul also informs us that God was pleased through the foolishness of what was preached to save those who believe.

For since in the wisdom of God the world through its wisdom did not know him, God was pleased through the foolishness of what was preached to save those who believe.

— *NIV, 1Cor. 1:21*

Paul informs us that the foolishness of God is wiser than the wisdom of men and that the weakness of God is stronger than the strength of men.

For the foolishness of God is wiser than man's wisdom, and the weakness of God is stronger than man's strength.

— *NIV, 1Cor. 1:25*

In verse 30, Paul says because of God, we are in Christ and Christ has become our righteousness, our holiness and our redemption.

It is because of him that you are in Christ Jesus, who has become for us wisdom from God—that is, our righteousness, holiness and redemption.

— *NIV, 1Cor. 1:30*

For I resolved to know nothing while I was with you except Jesus Christ and him crucified.

— *NIV, 1Cor. 2:2*

[1] Now, brothers, I want to remind you of the gospel I preached to you, which you received and on which you have taken your stand. [2] By this gospel you are saved, if you hold firmly to the word I preached to you. Otherwise, you have believed in vain. [3] For what I received I passed on to you as of first importance: that

Christ died for our sins according to the Scriptures, ⁴ that he was buried, that he was raised on the third day according to the Scriptures.

— *NIV, 1 Cor. 15:1-4*

Paul preached Christ crucified. In other words, Paul is saying that the weakness of God, which is preaching Christ crucified, will be so strong and powerful that this preaching will save those who believe. Can anyone truly believe without repenting? Those who truly believe are those who trust and repent; those who repent are both forgiven and saved. This is the wisdom and power of God. Sadly many would and still believe this is foolishness! I believe that it may be very helpful to take a closer look at a few verses recorded in 1 Corinthians. These verses are:

I am thankful that I did not baptize any of you except Crispus and Gaius,

— *NIV, 1 Cor. 1:14*

For Christ did not send me to baptize, but to preach the gospel— not with words of human wisdom, lest the cross of Christ be emptied of its power.

— *NIV, 1 Cor. 1:17*

Even though you have ten thousand guardians in Christ, you do not have many fathers, for in Christ Jesus I became your father through the gospel.

— *NIV, 1 Cor. 4:15*

I personally have never been able to understand how anyone could study these verses and then not realize that Paul was sent by Jesus to preach the gospel and was not sent to baptize. In my opinion, a distinction between baptism and preaching the gospel has plainly been made within these inspired written words of God through the Apostle Paul; "For Christ did not send me to baptize, but to preach the gospel."

My present understanding is that to argue this to be untrue would be nothing short of totally deliberate foolishness. What I understand and believe to be true is not as important as what you understand and believe to be true. My prayers are for you to pray and study God's written words and only then decide for yourself what is spiritual truth. You may or may not understand and believe as I do. Study and only then decide. The spiritual understanding and the spiritual light which we receive will prevent all of us from walking this life in spiritual darkness.

Paul was thankful that he had not baptized many of the Corinthian believers. Paul also informs them and us that Christ "did not send me to baptize, but to preach the gospel." Then in the fourth chapter, verse fifteen, Paul also informs the Corinthians and us that he had become their spiritual father through or by the gospel; Paul was their spiritual father and they were his spiritual children. Paul had begotten the Corinthians by preaching the Gospel, not by baptizing them. The Corinthians were spiritually born by faith and repentance, because of or by the powerful spiritual sword, which Paul had preached to them.

Even though you have ten thousand guardians in Christ, you do not have many fathers, for in Christ Jesus I became your father through the gospel.

— NIV, 1Cor. 4:15

Please ask yourself the following questions:
1. If baptism had saved these Corinthians, would Paul have been thankful that he had baptized only a few of them? (Please read that one again and think!)
2. Would Paul have written to the Corinthians and us that Christ sent him not to baptize but to preach the gospel?

Paul also informs the Corinthians that the same spirit spiritually baptized all of them into the same body.

For we were all baptized by one Spirit into one body—whether Jews or Greeks, slave or free—and we were all given the one Spirit to drink.

— NIV, 1Cor. 12:13

Once again, this is precisely what is recorded in the tenth chapter of Acts concerning Cornelius and his Gentile friends. They were spiritually baptized by the Holy Spirit into the spiritual body of Christ: His Church! Then they were physically baptized in water. Paul wrote First Corinthians around 55 A.D., many, many years after the conversion of Cornelius and his Gentile friends. Please realize that I do not want you to believe what I have stated is biblical truth. My desire is only for you to study God's word and then decide for yourself. We must realize that there are two baptisms, the first baptism is a spiritual baptism by the Holy Spirit and this baptism by the Spirit is the one baptism which places all of us into the spiritual body of Christ (Eph. 4:5 and 1Cor. 12:13). Then water baptism follows as an obedient act of faith and is a public testimony (Acts 10:48).

Paul's commission is recorded:

[17] Delivering thee from the people, and from the Gentiles, unto whom now I send thee, [18] To open their eyes, and to turn them from darkness to light, and from the power of Satan unto God, that they may receive forgiveness of sins, and inheritance among them which are sanctified by faith that is in me. [19] Whereupon, O king Agrippa, I was not disobedient unto the heavenly vision: [20] But showed first unto them of Damascus, and at Jerusalem, and throughout all the coasts of Judaea, and then to the Gentiles, that they should repent and turn to God, and do works meet for repentance.

— KJV, Acts 26:17-20

Paul's commission was "to open their eyes and turn them from darkness to light." To turn them from the power of Satan to the power of God. Paul was sent to preach Christ crucified, not to baptize. Paul preached that people should repent (Acts 26:20). Why? So they could receive forgiveness of their sins and inheritance among them who are sanctified by faith in Jesus (Acts 26:18). In my opinion, there should be no doubt that in these verses, which we have just studied, Paul has plainly made a distinction between baptism and preaching the gospel.

Once again I would like to remind you that what I believe to be true, may or may not be true. I encourage you to study Scripture and only then decide what you believe to be true to God's written word. I can imagine Paul preaching Christ crucified. All that we need to do is to search some of his Letters, which were inspired by the Holy Spirit. Paul also wrote the following inspired verses:

And you also were included in Christ when you heard the word of truth, the gospel of your salvation. Having believed, you were marked in him with a seal, the promised Holy Spirit.
— *NIV, Eph. 1:13*

God presented him as a sacrifice of atonement, through faith in his blood. He did this to demonstrate his justice, because in his forbearance he had left the sins committed beforehand unpunished
— *NIV, Rom. 3:25*

That if you confess with your mouth, "Jesus is Lord," and believe in your heart that God raised him from the dead, you will be saved. For it is with your heart that you believe and are justified, and it is with your mouth that you confess and are saved.
— *NIV, Rom. 10:9-10*

Once again, pieces of the whole, conforming to the whole! Saved by Faith. By preaching to all nations we could hear; by hearing we could believe; and by believing we could be justified through faith, by His grace. Is it possible to truly believe His testimony, which is called faith, and then, not fall to our knees in confession and repentance?

Who was delivered for our offences, and was raised again for our justification.
— *KJV, Rom. 4:25*

In what sense was Christ, "raised again for our justification"? My present understanding of the above verse is that His resurrection was necessary to prove and to provide assurance to His disciples that Jesus truly was the Son of God. It was necessary for the commitment and dedication that would be required of His disciples, especially the Apostles.

[27] Then he said to Thomas, "Put your finger here; see my hands. Reach out your hand and put it into my side. Stop doubting and believe." [28] Thomas said to him, "My Lord and my God!" [29] Then Jesus told him, "Because you have seen me, you have believed; blessed are those who have not seen and yet have believed."
                                                          — NIV, John 20: 27-29

They knew he had died; now they knew He was alive. Because they saw or witnessed His physical resurrected body, they would now be willing to forsake their own personal goals in life and willingly allow the Holy Spirit to use them physically. Preaching to all nations and also being used by the Holy Spirit to physically write the inspired words of the testimony of Christ. Just as Jesus willingly gave Himself, so would now his disciples and the Apostles. They would willingly die to self and live for Christ. The written word of God was dependent on their willingness to be lead and be used by the Holy Spirit.

The physical existence of the New Testament would ensure that the preaching of the gospel of Jesus Christ would continue for all ages. By preaching, we may hear; by hearing, we may believe. Justification is only possible by faith; faith is dependent upon believing; and one cannot believe if one has never heard. The physical existence of the New Testament we have today was only made possible by the physical efforts of the Apostles and the inspiration of the Holy Spirit. In this sense, "raised again for our justification," means, to ensure that we would hear, believe and be justified through faith. Faith in what? Faith in His blood for the remission of sins! God's Amazing Grace.

I believe that it would be helpful as well as necessary at this time to see what Scripture has revealed to us on this very controversial topic. I can think of no better place than the Epistle to the Ephesians, written by the apostle Paul. Most scholars date the writing of this letter around 60-62 A.D. They also believe that Paul was probably in prison at Rome when this letter was written. Ephesians is also thought to have been a circular letter, which means that it was sent to many other churches and not only to the Ephesians. The major theme of this letter is the body of Christ, His Church. God had revealed a mystery to Paul and now God had decided to reveal this mystery to those who have ears to hear and eyes to see. Spiritual light; spiritual understanding given by His Glorious Light: His Son.

Chapter 11

The Mystery

¹ For this reason I, Paul, the prisoner of Christ Jesus for the sake of you Gentiles— ² Surely you have heard about the administration of God's grace that was given to me for you, ³ that is, the mystery made known to me by revelation, as I have already written briefly. ⁴ In reading this, then, you will be able to understand my insight into the mystery of Christ, ⁵ which was not made known to men in other generations as it has now been revealed by the Spirit to God's holy apostles and prophets. ⁶ This mystery is that through the gospel the Gentiles are heirs together with Israel, members together of one body, and sharers together in the promise in Christ Jesus.

— NIV, Eph. 3:1-6

In the above inspired verses from Paul, we read, "the mystery made known to me by revelation, as I have already written briefly. In reading this, then, you will be able to understand my insight into the mystery of Christ." Now, let's turn back to the two previous chapters and read Paul's insight into the mystery of Christ, which he had already written about.

⁶ to the praise of his glorious grace, which he has freely given us in the One he loves. ⁷ In him we have redemption through his blood, the forgiveness of sins, in accordance with the riches of God's grace ⁸ that he lavished on us with all wisdom and understanding. ⁹ And he made known to us the mystery of his will according to his good pleasure, which he purposed in Christ, ¹⁰ *to be put into effect when the times will have reached their fulfillment—to bring all things in heaven and on earth together under one head, even Christ.* ¹¹ *In him we were also chosen, having been predestined according to the plan of him who works out everything in conformity with the purpose of his will,* ¹² *in order that we, who were the first to hope in Christ, might be for the praise of his glory.* ¹³ *And you also were included in Christ when you heard the word of truth, the gospel of your salvation. Having believed, you were marked in him with a seal, the promised Holy Spirit,* ¹⁴ *who is a deposit guaranteeing our inheritance until the redemption of those who are God's possession—to the praise of his glory.* ¹⁵ *For this reason, ever since I heard about your faith in the Lord Jesus and your love for all the saints,* ¹⁶ *I have not stopped giving thanks for you, remembering you in my prayers.*

— NIV, Eph. 1:6-16

¹ *As for you, you were dead in your transgressions and sins,* ² *in which you used to live when you followed the ways of this world and of the ruler of the kingdom of the air, the spirit who is now at work in those who are disobedient.* ³ *All of us also lived among them at one time, gratifying the cravings of our sinful nature and following its desires and thoughts. Like the rest, we were by nature objects of wrath.* ⁴ *But because of his great love for us, God, who is rich in mercy,* ⁵ *made us alive with Christ even when we were dead in transgressions—it is by grace you have been saved.* ⁶ *And God raised us up with Christ and seated us with him in the heavenly realms in Christ Jesus,* ⁷ *in order that in the coming ages he might show the incomparable riches of his grace, expressed in his kindness to us in Christ Jesus.* ⁸ *For it is by grace you have been saved, through faith—and this not from yourselves, it is the gift of God—* ⁹ *not by works, so that no one can boast.* ¹⁰ *For we are God's workmanship, created in Christ Jesus to do good works, which God prepared in advance for us to do.*

— NIV, Eph. 2:1-10

[17] He came and preached peace to you who were far away and peace to those who were near. [18] For through him we both have access to the Father by one Spirit.
— NIV, Eph. 2:17-18

[6] This mystery is that through the gospel the Gentiles are heirs together with Israel, members together of one body, and sharers together in the promise in Christ Jesus. [7] I became a servant of this gospel by the gift of God's grace given me through the working of his power. [8] Although I am less than the least of all God's people, this grace was given me: to preach to the Gentiles the unsearchable riches of Christ, [9] and to make plain to everyone the administration of this mystery, which for ages past was kept hidden in God, who created all things. [10] His intent was that now, through the church, the manifold wisdom of God should be made known to the rulers and authorities in the heavenly realms, [11] according to his eternal purpose which he accomplished in Christ Jesus our Lord. [12] In him and through faith in him we may approach God with freedom and confidence.
— NIV, Eph. 3:6-12

[16] I pray that out of his glorious riches he may strengthen you with power through his Spirit in your inner being, so that Christ may dwell in your hearts through faith. [17] And I pray that you, being rooted and established in love, [18] may have power, together with all the saints, to grasp how wide and long and high and deep is the love of Christ, [19] and to know this love that surpasses knowledge—that you may be filled to the measure of all the fullness of God.
— NIV, Eph. 3:16-19

[4] There is one body and one Spirit— just as you were called to one hope when you were called— [5] one Lord, one faith, one baptism
— NIV, Eph. 4:4

Again, this is exactly what is recorded in the Book of Acts concerning Cornelius and his Gentile friends (Acts 10:43-45). They did not receive the Holy Spirit by any Jewish ritual nor had they received the Holy Spirit by any Christian ordinance such as baptism! They had received the Holy Spirit by faith!

[13] "And you also were included in Christ when you heard the word of truth, the gospel of your salvation. Having believed, you were marked in him with a seal, the promised Holy Spirit, [14] who is a deposit guaranteeing our inheritance until the redemption of those who are God's possession—to the praise of his glory."

— NIV, Eph. 1:13-14

[15] "For you did not receive a spirit that makes you a slave again to fear, but you received the Spirit of sonship. And by him we cry, 'Abba, Father.' [16] The Spirit himself testifies with our spirit that we are God's children."

— NIV, Rom. 8:15-16

Please remember that most scholars believe that Ephesians was written between 60 to 62 A. D. This was about ten years after the first church council meeting (50 A.D.) and about twenty years after the conversion of Cornelius.

"This mystery is that through the gospel the Gentiles are heirs together with Israel, members together of one body, and sharers together in the promise in Christ Jesus."

— NIV, Eph. 3:6

[6] "to the praise of his glorious grace, which he has freely given us in the One he loves. [7] In him we have redemption through his blood, the forgiveness of sins, in accordance with the riches of God's grace

— NIV, Eph. 1:6-7

123

"For through him we both have access to the Father by one Spirit."

— *NIV, Eph. 2:18*

"For it is by grace you have been saved, through faith—and this not from yourselves, it is the gift of God—not by works, so that no one can boast."

— *NIV, Eph. 2:8-9*

According to Paul: "There is one body and one Spirit—just as you were called to one hope when you were called—one Lord, one faith, one baptism" (NIV, Eph. 4:4-5).

There is one body and there is one baptism according to Paul. When we think of baptism we realize that there are two different baptisms. One is a physical water baptism performed by the hands of men, the other is a spiritual baptism performed by the Holy Spirit. Therefore we should search Scripture allowing Scripture to inform us which baptism places us in the body of Christ. We need not to go far to receive spiritual light and understanding.

He redeemed us in order that the blessing given to Abraham might come to the Gentiles through Christ Jesus, so that by faith we might receive the promise of the Spirit.

— *NIV, Gal. 3:14*

For we were all baptized by one Spirit into one body—whether Jews or Greeks, slave or free—and we were all given the one Spirit to drink.

— *NIV, 1Cor. 12:13*

The Spirit himself testifies with our spirit that we are God's children.

— *NIV, Rom. 8:16*

[15] I have written you quite boldly on some points, as if to remind you of them again, because of the grace God gave me [16] to be a minister of Christ Jesus to the Gentiles with the priestly duty of

proclaiming the gospel of God, so that the Gentiles might become an offering acceptable to God, sanctified by the Holy Spirit.
— *NIV, Rom. 15:15-16*

[13] *"And you also were included in Christ when you heard the word of truth, the gospel of your salvation. Having believed, you were marked in him with a seal, the promised Holy Spirit,* [14] *who is a deposit guaranteeing our inheritance until the redemption of those who are God's possession—to the praise of his glory."*
— *NIV, Eph. 1:13-14*

We easily see that the one baptism which places us into the body of Christ is a spiritual baptism by the Holy Spirit (1 Cor. 12:13), not a baptism in water done by the hands of men. We truly need nobody. Nobody, except Jesus!

Chapter 12

Baptismal Regeneration

What is it? What does it mean? You may be asking yourself, *why is he going to write about Baptismal Regeneration?* Well, I have already informed you that I am not a scholar, now I would like to share with you some personal information about myself. Not only am I not a scholar, I never finished high school. I did finish the tenth grade though. Now wait just a minute before you close this book and try to get your money back. If I had given you this information in the beginning, would you have read this book to this page? Decisions. Life is full of them.

My reason for writing about baptismal regeneration truly is a personal one. My family and I spent almost ten wonderful years serving and worshipping our Lord and Savior in a church which believes in baptismal regeneration. I remember how amazed we were the first time we attended Sunday morning service. The love shown to our family is beyond words. We gave ourselves time to become familiar with their beliefs and their teachings. We attended services for two years before we became members. During those two years, we had not heard the term "baptismal regeneration" once. Our involvement in this church was not Sunday morning dusting of the pews, as we sat down for services.

My wife Cindy, whom I personally believe to be a blessing to me from God, taught Sunday school for eight years and considered her class to be both a privilege and a blessing. I served seven years as a deacon and board member. Together, Cindy and I were youth directors of the children and teens of the church. This ministry was considered by both of us to be our highest privilege and blessing. Our relationship with the members of our church was closer than our relationships with some of our biological family members. We were blessed to have our minister and his wife as our closest friends.

Yes, Christians can play cards; we certainly did, and all of us really enjoyed it too. But to be perfectly honest, our minister's wife, who was always my card partner, was not a very good card partner, to say the least. She was my partner in Spades for five years and she is still trying to learn how to play the game. Life was pretty good and we felt that we were where we should be, doing what we should be doing. We truly believed that this was the Lord's will for the two of us. Then one Sunday morning, my closest friend, our minister, said the following words during his sermon; "Salvation is that moment when we are baptized; for the remission of our sins, and not before we are baptized."

Now I am not bragging in any way here, I am only being honest. I have never been one to fall asleep during a sermon. The words, which are spoken from the pulpit or any other place or any other time, are to be the true words of God and not the words of men. I always listen to every word and believe this to be the responsibility of all Christians. The reason for this follows.

All Scripture is God-breathed and is useful for teaching, rebuking, correcting and training in righteousness, so that the man of God may be thoroughly equipped for every good work. In the presence of God and of Christ Jesus, who will judge the living and the dead, and in view of his appearing and his kingdom, I give you this charge: Preach the Word; be prepared in season and out of season; correct, rebuke and encourage— with great patience and careful instruction. For the time will come when men will not put up with sound doctrine. Instead, to suit their own desires, they will gather around them a great number of teachers to say what their itching ears want to hear. They will turn their ears away from the truth and turn aside to myths. But you,

keep your head in all situations, endure hardship, do the work of an evangelist, discharge all the duties of your ministry
— *NIV, 2 Tim. 3:16-4:5*

For the message of the cross is foolishness to those who are perishing, but to us who are being saved it is the power of God.
— *NIV, 1Cor. 1:18*

The foolishness of God is wiser, than the wisdom of men (1Cor. 1:25). The foolishness of God is that; "it pleased God by the foolishness of preaching to save them that believe (1Cor. 1:21). My present understanding is that the true "message of the gospel" is "that everyone who believes in him receives forgiveness of sins through his name"(Acts 10:43). This is why God has commanded men everywhere to repent.

In the past God overlooked such ignorance, but now he commands all people everywhere to repent.
— *NIV, Acts 17:30*

This message is both the power and wisdom of God, which gives the gift of salvation to all who believe this message and repent. The destiny of many souls is at stake! This is why it is so important for all of us to listen and also to give a great amount of thought and discernment to what is being preached to us and to the world.

After church that morning, I thought that it might be a good idea to visit my best friend, our minister, the following day. Well to make a long story short, what I had thought to have been said turned out to be what had been said. We were both in shock. Neither one of us could believe that I had never heard these words before. The fact that my work schedule prevents me from being able to be in church every Sunday was more than likely the main reason for this. After a very lengthy discussion, we decided that the Elders should be informed. To make a longer story shorter, seven months later and only after a great amount of prayer and many family discussions, we decided that the right thing to do would be to leave our church. I am unable to tell you how difficult this decision was.

I believe when God closes one door, He always has another door open for His children. My family and I can testify to this first hand. During those seven months, we had contacted several local churches of various denominations and had felt that the Lord was leading us to a local Church of the Nazarene. We decided to leave our church and began worshipping at the Church of the Nazarene. Four months later and only after many hours of theological discussions with the pastor, we decided to become members of the Church of the Nazarene. In a short time, my wife was privileged and blessed once again to be a Sunday school teacher. Shortly after that, we were both blessed again with the privilege of being permitted to teach the teens of our new church on Sunday evenings.

We have been attending our new church for two years and continue to love and see many members of our previous church. We have reasons to believe that this will always continue to be true. Along the side of love, there also stands respect, this love and respect will never fade away. This respect is a respect for each other's commitment to their present understanding of Scripture. Disagreement should not destroy respect for one's commitment to Christ. Disagreement should never destroy or even harm Christian love for each other. I am writing about baptismal regeneration because of love. Love for my Lord and Savior and also because of the love, which my wife and I have in our hearts for our dear friends who believe in baptismal regeneration.

Our decision to worship at a different church has not prevented the continuous growth of our love for our friends at our previous church. Their commitment to Christ deserves and has our respect, regardless of our disagreements of what Scripture requires for salvation. They believe that they understand Scripture correctly, just as my wife and I believe that our present understanding of Scripture is correct. They love the Lord and serve Him, just as my wife and I love the Lord and serve Him to the best of our abilities. Our place of worship has changed; however their place in our hearts will never change.

Our new church family has shown us nothing except pure Christian love. Our appreciation could never be fully expressed by words. We have been blessed by their love and kindness and praise God for their spiritual maturity. We truly believe that when God closes one door, God always has a purpose for closing that door; God will always have another door waiting. In my mind the key to open any door to spiritual blessings is called "obedience." The blessings are provided by God, however the key of obedience enables the blessings to be a reality. My wife and I both lift up our praises to Him, for His love, guidance, blessings and His unmerited amazing grace.

I suppose the easiest way to explain baptismal regeneration is as follows: Baptismal regeneration is the understanding and belief that water baptism is necessary for salvation. That God's grace is given: by God only when an individual is baptized with water for the remission of sins. Some supporters of baptismal regeneration believe immersion is necessary, while others believe sprinkling is sufficient.

The Internet is a very valuable tool available to Christians everywhere. Information is now accessible at the tip of our fingers, though it was not available to many people only a decade ago. I was amazed to discover that so many different denominations believe and teach baptismal regeneration. In the beginning of this book, I stated that I had no desire to accuse anyone of anything. For this reason, I personally, will not list the names of various denominations, which teach baptismal regeneration.

The history of baptismal regeneration extends back to the second century. I believe that you are aware of the theology and teachings of your church. I do feel that it is appropriate for me to inform you of the name of the church which my family and I dealt with. Their name is The Christian Church. They trace their roots back to the 1800s to two main gentlemen named Alexander and Thomas Campbell. Thomas Campbell came to this country and began ministering to congregations in Western Pennsylvania in 1807. His son Alexander Campbell was born September 12, 1788 in Ireland.

Alexander came to this country and became the pastor of a Presbyterian church in Washington County, Pennsylvania, in 1809. He soon became dissatisfied with the Presbyterian denomination. In

1810, he and his father founded and became the main leaders of a new religious society at Brush Run, Pennsylvania. Alexander had been baptized when he was an infant by sprinkling. Over the years, Alexander had spent a great amount of time studying the subject of infant baptism. He came to the proper conclusion that repentance must precede baptism. He also came to the conviction that immersion was the proper scriptural mode for baptism. I stated that I have no desire to make accusations. For this reason, I will only present writings from the Christian Churches and their Restoration Movement writers. My desire is to allow their writers to provide us with information. I believe that it would be both inappropriate and unfair to use the writings of those who oppose their doctrine of baptismal regeneration.

* * * *

The following section has been a heavy burden for me. When I first completed this section, I struggled with the decision of removing it. I decided to remove it from the book and did so. As I continued to write, I could not forget my feeling of responsibility to provide you with information. My prayer is that my decision to inform you will not be thought of as a desire to criticize. I believe that accurate information is a valuable asset which all individuals have a privileged right of access to. I sincerely pray that after you have read the following section, your opinion will be that it has been presented in an informative, proper and respectful way. I apologize to all who may come to the opinion that this goal was not achieved by me.

* * * *

On June 12, 1812, Alexander Campbell and six others were baptized by Matthias Luce. The following words are from Alexander Campbell. Mr. Richardson asked Mr. Campbell, "Were you not baptized by a Regular Baptist and in a Regular Baptist way?"

"I was immersed by a Regular Baptist but not in a Regular Baptist way. I stipulated with Matthias Luce that I should be immersed on the profession of the one fact or proposition that Jesus was the Messiah, the Son of God. When I solicited his attendance with me on that occasion he replied that it was not usual for Baptists to immerse simply on that profession but he believed it to be scriptural. Fearing, however, to be called to account for it by some of his brethren he solicited the attendance of Henry Spears."[7]

From the above statement made by Campbell in 1831, Mr. Campbell said, "I should be immersed on the profession of the one fact or proposition that Jesus was the Messiah, the Son of God." In others words, he was baptized on June 12th, 1812, on the simple confession that Jesus Christ was the Son of God. He was not baptized for the remission of sins. Matthias Luce had never baptized anyone only on that simple confession and he was fearful that his Baptist brothers might call on him to explain why he had done so. Because of his fear of accountability, Matthias Luce "solicited the attendance of Henry Spears." The Baptists at this time required a testimony from what they referred to as the "mourners bench" followed by a vote of acceptance and approval.

The point their own writers will show is that the founding fathers of the Restoration Movement were not baptized for the remission of sins. When I first realized that on June 12, 1812, a historical day in the Restoration Movement, that Mr. Campbell had not been baptized for the remission of sins, I decided to attempt to find additional information. I wanted to know if Mr. Campbell had ever been baptized for the remission of sins. This decision provided me with the following information.

This is what Mr. Campbell believed almost eleven and a half years after Matthias Luce had baptized him! In 1823, Mr. Campbell made the following statement: "The blood of Christ, then, really cleanses us who believe from all sin. Behold the goodness of God in giving us a formal proof and token of it, by ordaining a baptism expressly 'for the remission of sins!' The water of baptism, then, formally washes away our sins. The blood of Christ really washes away our sins. Paul's sins were really pardoned when he believed, yet he had no solemn pledge of the fact, no formal acquittal, no formal purgation of his sins, until he washed them away in the water of baptism."[8]

Then in 1829, Mr. Campbell made the following statement: "Knowing that the efficacy of this blood is to be communicated to our consciences in the way which God has pleased to appoint, we 'stagger not at the promises of God' but flee to the sacred ordinance which brings the blood of Jesus in contact with our consciences. Without knowing and believing this, immersion is as empty as a blasted nut. The shell is there, but the kernel is wanting."[9]

I will not share with you my thoughts about these two statements. I will only ask you to ask yourself the following questions.

1. What is the difference between "really" & "formally"?
2. Does Scripture ask us to have faith in His blood for the remission of sins? (Mat. 26:28, Rom. 3:25 and Heb. 10:19-22)
3. Is God's written word a "solemn pledge"
4. If "Paul's sins were really pardoned when he believed" and if "the blood of Christ then really cleanses us who believe from all sin," would Paul or anyone need to "formally wash away our sins" with "the water of baptism"?

Then in 1843, Campbell made the following statement. "Some twenty years ago, when preparing for a debate with Mr. McCalla, I put myself under the special instruction of four Evangelists, and one Paul, of distinguished apostolic rank and dignity. I had some time before that discussion, been often impressed with such passages as Acts 2:38; and that providential call to discuss the subject with Mr. McCalla, compelled me to decide the matter to my entire satisfaction. Believe me, Sir then I had forgotten my earlier readings upon the subject: and upon the simple testimony of the Book itself, I came to a conclusion alleged in that debate, and proved only by the Bible which now appears, from a thousand sources, to have been the catholic and truly ancient and primitive faith of the whole church. It was in this commonwealth that this doctrine was first promulgated in modern times: and, sir, it has now spread over this continent, and with singular success is now returning to Europe, and the land of our fathers."[10]

These statements by Mr. Campbell inform us that in 1823, in the Campbell-McCalla Debate, Mr. Campbell had decided to his entire satisfaction that Acts 2:38 was to be understood, that we must be literally baptized for the remission of sins.

In Volume 2, page 217, of *The Memoirs of Alexander Campbell*, Mr. Campbell is quoted as saying, "I put baptism for remission of sins in my creed in 1823, but did not begin to practice it for some time afterward."

After I had read this information, I was forced by logical thinking to ask myself the following question. *Why not?* In 1823, he had decided to his entire satisfaction on this baptismal regeneration doctrine. However this information did not answer my question. I continued my search and found the following. On page 32 of J. N. Hall's *Campbellite Catechism* is published an article from the *Gospel Advocate,* Dec. 2, 1897, which was written by T. R. Burnett. "Alexander Campbell and Walter Scott, and John Smith and Jacob Creath and all the pioneers were immersed before they learned that baptism was for remission of sins. Walter Scott baptized William Amend on Nov. 18, 1827, 'for the remission of sins,' and he was the first person in modern times to baptized. This was fifteen years after the baptism of Alexander Campbell and his father, Thomas Campbell, which occurred at Brush Run in 1812. Neither one of those gentlemen had baptized a believer in order to obtain remission of sins during those fifteen years."

This is a very important historical fact, which should be known by all people, especially by all members of the Restoration Movement. The recorded history of the Restoration Movement, written by their own writers, proves the undeniable truth that Alexander Campbell, Thomas Campbell, Walter Scott and Barton Stone were never baptized "for the forgiveness of sins." Therefore, according to their very own doctrine, which they adamantly hold to, proclaim and preach, their very own founding fathers of their Restoration Movement are not the children of God! This is a historical fact.

Their own doctrine and theology places their founding fathers among those who are lost and unsaved. They would be, according to their own theology, children of Satan!

The following quote is also from Mr. Alexander Campbell. "We flatter ourselves that the principles are now clearly and fully developed by the united efforts of a few devoted and ardent minds, who set out determined to sacrifice everything to truth, and follow her wherever she might lead the way: I say, the principles on which the church of Jesus Christ—all believers in Jesus as the Messiah—can be united with honor to themselves, and with blessings to the world; on which the gospel and its ordinances can be restored in all their primitive simplicity, excellency, and power, and the church shine as a lamp that burneth to the conviction and salvation of the world:—I say, the principles by which these things can be done are now developed, as well as the principles themselves, which together constitute the original gospel and order of things established by the Apostles."[11]

After reading and studying the above quotation from Mr. Campbell, there is no need in my opinion to discuss the word modesty ("We flatter ourselves"). We can easily realize from these words that Mr. Campbell believed that: (1) the Gospel was restored, (2) the Ordinances were restored, and (3) the Church was restored.

All of this was done, according to Mr. Campbell, "by the united efforts of a few devoted and ardent minds."

Whether you believe this to be true or not is your decision. There is no need for me to make a comment. My desire is only to provide you with accurate information, using only their very own writers. Again, I believe that you are very capable of making your own decision, once you have the historical information at hand. Once again, my desire is to inform not to accuse or criticize. However, the undeniable truth is that the founding fathers of the Restoration Movement were never baptized "for" (to receive) the forgiveness of sins. This being a historical fact, I believe that the following question requires some serious thought.

If the Gospel, the Ordinances and the Church were actually restored by these individuals, would this then mean that God used unsaved sinners for their restoration?

While I was doing my research for this book, I discovered a truly remarkable article written by Alexander Campbell, on the 12th of April 1829 and titled *The Three Kingdoms.*

"THE Jewish people were often called "the kingdom of God," because God was in a peculiar sense their King. For certain purposes he selected them, distinguished them, and took them under his own immediate protection. He gave them laws, ordinances, and customs, which had both a specific and general influence, and were preparatory to a new and better order of society. The new order of society which arises out of the belief of the gospel, is often called "the reign or kingdom of Heaven." In this kingdom the subjects enjoy more exalted blessings, and stand in new and heavenly relations unknown before the coming of the Messiah.— There is also the "kingdom of heaven, or glory," properly so called. This is the residence of angels, the abode of the saints, and the mansions of glory. The gates of admission into these three kingdoms are different—Flesh, Faith, and Works. To be born of the flesh, or to be a descendant of Abraham, introduced a child into the first kingdom of God. To be born of water and spirit, through faith in Jesus Christ, brings men and women into the second kingdom. But neither flesh, faith, nor water, without good works, will introduce a man or woman into the third kingdom. The nature of these three kingdoms, the privileges enjoyed by the subjects, and the terms of admission, are very imperfectly understood in the present day. These kingdoms are unhappily confounded in the minds of many. Hence we find that what is affirmed of the nature, subjects, and terms of admission of one, is frequently applied to another. This is one of the roots of popery, and all the hierarchies in christendom have sprung from it.

The nature of the kingdom of God amongst the Jews is very different from the nature of the kingdom of God amongst the christians, and both are different from the kingdom of glory.—The subjects are just as different. Under the first they were carnal; all the descendants of Jacob, without regard to regeneration, were lawful subjects of the first kingdom. None can be subjects of the second unless born again; and flesh and blood cannot inherit the third and ultimate kingdom.

I have discovered that the objections offered against the scriptural design and import of christian immersion, are based upon a misapprehension of the nature and privileges of these three kingdoms. Under the first there were various ablutions, purgations, and sin-offerings, which never perfected the conscience; but which, for the time being, served as symbols or types of a real purgation which would be enjoyed under the Reign of Heaven, or second kingdom.—These sacrifices did not cleanse the worshippers, else, as Paul reasons, the worshippers, once cleansed, would have no more consciousness of sins. Under the christian economy a real remission of sins is constantly enjoyed by all the subjects or citizens, and, as Paul argues, where remission of sins is enjoyed no more sacrifice for sin is needed. Now if the Jews by faith foresaw through the symbols the shedding of Christ's blood, the question is, Why could they not by faith in his sacrifice enjoy, as well as we, the remission of sins? The sacrifice of Christ, viewed prospectively, was as efficacious as when viewed retrospectively, to effect the cleansing of the conscience. And could they not, through one sacrifice, have more clearly understood the design of Christ's sacrifice, than by so many sacrifices. But it is a provision in the constitution of the christian kingdom which greatly distinguishes it from the Jewish, "that the sins and iniquities of the citizens shall be remembered no more." No daily, weekly, nor annual remembrances of sins under the reign of favor. This, faith in the sacrifice of Christ discovers, and submission to his institution puts us into the actual possession of that remission which never was enjoyed before.

Now, as Paul teaches, under the Constitution of the New Kingdom, remission of sins is a natural birthright. Hence every one, so soon as he enters the second or christian kingdom, or is born of water and spirit, is pardoned and accepted. So that those who are born into the kingdom of heaven, or christian kingdom, have peace with God, and sin cannot lord it over them; for they are not under law, but under favor.

But many say, "What will become of our Paidobaptist brethren, and millions more, if these things be so?" This is a stale objection which has been urged against every reformation in religion from the days of John Huss down to this century. I will, however, answer the interrogatory. They cannot enjoy the blessings of the second kingdom; in other words, they can not have or enjoy that light, peace, liberty, and love, which are the national privileges of all who intelligently enter the kingdom of favor.

But the objector means, Can they enter into the third kingdom, or kingdom of glory? I am prepared to say that my opinion is, and it is but an opinion, that infants, idiots, and some Jews and

*Pagans may, without either faith or baptism, be
brought into the third kingdom, merely in
consequence of the sacrifice of Christ; and I
doubt not but many Paidobaptists of all sects will
be admitted into the kingdom of glory.—*

*Indeed all they who obey Jesus Christ, through
faith in his blood, according to their knowledge, I
am of opinion will be introduced into that
kingdom. But when we talk of the forgiveness of
sins which comes to christians through immersion,
we have no regard to any other than the second
kingdom, or the kingdom of favor. I repeat it
again—there are three kingdoms: the Kingdom of
Law, the Kingdom of Favor, and the Kingdom of
Glory; each has a different constitution, different
subjects, privileges, and terms of admission. And
who is so blind, in the Christian kingdom, as not
to see that more is necessary to eternal salvation
or to admission into the everlasting kingdom, than
either faith, regeneration, or immersion? A man
can enter into the second kingdom by being born
of water and the spirit; but he cannot enter into
the third and ultimate kingdom through faith,
immersion, or regeneration. Hence says the
Judge, Come you blessed of my Father, and
inherit the kingdom of glory. Because you
believed? No. Because you were immersed? No.
Because you were born again by the Holy Spirit?
No—but because I know your good works, your
piety, and humanity. I was hungry, and you fed
me.*

*The plain state of the case is this:—The blood of
Abraham brought a man into the kingdom of law,
and gave him an inheritance in Canaan. Being
born not of blood, but through water and the*

139

Spirit of God, brings a person into the kingdom of favor; which is righteousness, peace, joy, and a holy spirit, with a future inheritance in prospect. But if the justified draw back, or the washed return to the mire, or if faith die and bring forth no fruits—into the kingdom of glory he cannot enter. Hence good works through faith, or springing from faith in Jesus, give a right to enter into the holy city—and this is a right springing from grace or favor.—"Blessed are they who keep his commandments that they may have a right to the tree of life and enter through the gates into the city." This right, as observed, springs from a constitution of favor. And while men are saved by grace, or brought into the second kingdom, (for all in it are said to be saved in the New Testament style) by favor, they cannot enter the heavenly kingdom, but by patient continuance in well doing. So stands the decree of the Lord Almighty as I understand the Oracles.

Those who desire the enjoyment of remission of sins, peace with God, and abundance of joy, can obtain them through submission to an institution of pure favor, as already defined. But when we speak of admission into the everlasting kingdom, we must have a due respect to those grand and fundamental principles so clearly propounded in the New Institution. We must discriminate between the kingdom of favor, and the kingdom of glory."[12]

In all honesty, when I first read this article I did not read it once, I read it four or five times. Since then, I have read this article many more times. The more I read this article, the more my head spins. I like to refer to this article as "The Article of Theology, by Alexander

Campbell." I will not pretend to understand everything in this article, I will only share with you what I presently understand.

According to Mr. Campbell's theology, there are three kingdoms. "The Kingdom of Law, The Kingdom of Favor and The Kingdom of Glory." Each kingdom has a different constitution, different subjects, different privileges and different terms of admission. "The gates of admission into these three kingdoms are also different." I will attempt to explain these three kingdoms as clearly as possible. My desire is to use only Campbell's own words whenever possible, because according to Campbell, "the privileges enjoyed by the subjects, and the terms of admission, are very imperfectly understood in the present day."[13]

We will begin with the Jewish kingdom, the Kingdom of Law. Campbell calls the gate of admission "Flesh." Flesh to be born of the flesh is to be a descendant of Abraham. "All the descendants of Jacob, without regard to regeneration, were lawful subjects of the first kingdom."

"None can be subjects of the second unless born again; and flesh and blood cannot inherit the third and ultimate kingdom." However, Campbell says, "I am prepared to say that my opinion is, and it is but an opinion, that infants, idiots, and some Jews and Pagans may, without either faith or baptism, be brought into the third kingdom, merely in consequence of the sacrifice of Christ;"

The second kingdom, Campbell refers to as The Kingdom of Favor. Campbell refers to the gate of admission to this second kingdom as "Faith." According to Campbell, there is no remission of sins without baptism.

I have discovered that the objections offered against the scriptural design and import of Christian immersion, are based upon a misapprehension of the nature and privileges of these three kingdoms ... None can be subjects of the second unless born again ... This faith in the sacrifice of Christ discovers, and submission to

*his institution puts us into the actual possession of
that remission which never was enjoyed before ...
To be born of water and spirit, through faith in
Jesus Christ, brings men and women into the
second kingdom ... But when we talk of the
forgiveness of sins which comes to Christians
through immersion, we have no regard to any
other than the second kingdom, or the kingdom of
favor ... Hence every one, so soon as he enters
the second or Christian kingdom, or is born of
water and spirit, is pardoned and accepted.*

The third kingdom, Campbell also refers to as The Kingdom of
Glory.

*But when we speak of admission into the
everlasting kingdom, we must have a due respect
to those grand and fundamental principles so
clearly propounded in the New Institution. We
must discriminate between the kingdom of favor,
and the kingdom of glory ... But neither flesh,
faith, nor water, without good works, will
introduce a man or woman into the third kingdom
... A man can enter into the second kingdom by
being born of water and the spirit; but he cannot
enter into the third and ultimate kingdom through
faith, immersion, or regeneration. Hence says the
Judge, Come you blessed of my Father, and
inherit the kingdom of glory. Because you
believed? No. Because you were immersed? No.
Because you were born again by the Holy Spirit?
No—but because I know your good works, your
piety, and humanity. I was hungry, and you fed
me, &c." And while men are saved by grace, or
brought into the second kingdom, (for all in it are*

> *said to be saved in the New Testament style) by*
> *favor, they cannot enter the heavenly kingdom,*
> *but by patient continuance in well doing. So*
> *stands the decree of the Lord Almighty as I*
> *understand the Oracles ... I repeat it again—there*
> *are three kingdoms: the Kingdom of Law, the*
> *Kingdom of Favor, and the Kingdom of Glory;*
> *each has a different constitution, different*
> *subjects, privileges, and terms of admission.*

To simplify Campbell's theology even further:

The First Kingdom —— The Kingdom of Law.
Admission Gate: Flesh.
Terms of admission:
1.   Heredity.

The Second Kingdom —— The Kingdom of Favor.
Admission Gate: Faith.
Terms of admission:
1.   "The scriptural design and import of Christian immersion" -
Baptized for the remission of sins.

The Third Kingdom —— The Kingdom of Glory.
Admission Gate: Works.
Terms of admission:
1.   "The scriptural design and import of Christian immersion" -
Baptized for the remission of sins.
2.   Good works.

My goal is to provide information, not criticism; therefore, I will not share with you my comments on Campbell's theology of his three kingdoms. I am confident that you have the ability to know if Campbell's theology is correct or incorrect according Scripture. The right to decide belongs to you! I would like to share one additional piece of information with you concerning Mr. Campbell and Daniel's 2300 Days. In 1832, in the Millennial Harbinger, Mr. Campbell wrote:

> *Now this question is of peculiar easy solution, for no event in history is more notorious than the battle at the rive Grandicus, in which Alexander the Great, the first king of the Grecian Empire, triumphed over Darius and, broke to pieces the Medo-Persian dynasty. Now we cannot date the Grecian Empire under the symbol of the 'goat', (which, by the way, was the ensign armorial of the Macedonian people), more correctly than from the invasion of Asia by Alexander and his all-conquering army, in the year before Christ 334. Here, then, we are compelled, by force of historic facts, to date the vision under consideration. From this date we compute the 2300 days. And what is the result? The time of the end will be in the year of our Lord 1966—one hundred and twenty-three years yet distant. If, then, the Millerites, and all who agree with them in their times and seasons, seek to rid themselves of all the previous difficulties by taking the date of the vision proper, to which the 2300 days belong, if they prefer this horn of the dilemma, it is not as evident as demonstration that they have wholly mistaken the dates, (to say nothing more), and that which they are now expecting in 1843, can not occur till 1966.*

This question was "of peculiar easy solution" according to Mr. Campbell. To use only the words of Mr. Campbell: "we are compelled, by force of historic facts." "And what is the result?" "wholly mistaken." There is no doubt in my mind that Mr. Campbell was well aware of the following words, which were spoken by Jesus.

But of that day and hour knoweth no man, no, not the angels of heaven, but my Father only.

— *KJV, Mat. 24:36*

Believing that Mr. Campbell's awareness of this verse is a true fact, I am then forced to the logical conclusion that Mr. Campbell must not have believed these words to be true. In all honestly, any other conclusion is far beyond my personal comprehension "to say nothing more."

History has shown that the Apostle Peter was wrong (Gal. 2:11-14). History has now also shown that Mr. Campbell was wrong concerning the second coming of Christ. Is it then possible that Mr. Campbell's theology and understanding of the three kingdoms and their terms of admission are also wrong? Could his understanding of baptismal regeneration also be wrong?

The theology of baptismal regeneration is the belief and understanding that forgiveness of sins is only possible when we are baptized literally "for the remission of sins." The verse which is considered by many to be the backbone of baptismal regeneration theology follows.

Then Peter said unto them, Repent, and be baptized every one of you in the name of Jesus Christ for the remission of sins, and ye shall receive the gift of the Holy Ghost.

— *KJV, Acts 2:38*

My desire is to explain the use of this Greek preposition in an uncomplicated and easy to understand way. For this reason, I will compare the Greek preposition "Eis" with our English word "For." In Acts 2:38, eis is translated as for: "for the remission of sins." The Greek preposition eis may be used in two different ways. One way which eis may be used is: To express purpose or goal. In other words, in order to receive. Another way which eis may be used is: On the basis of. In other words, because of.

Our English word "for" is very similar to eis. A simple way to explain the usage of both eis and for is: to express purpose or goal. In other words, in order to receive. Examples of purpose or goal are: I pray (eis or for) blessings from God. In other words: I pray (to receive) blessings from God. I study (eis or for) knowledge. In other words: I study (to receive) knowledge. I pray (eis or for) wisdom. In other words: I pray (to receive) wisdom.

Another way, which both eis and for may be used is: On the basis of. In other words, because of. Examples of, "on the basis of," or "because of" are: I bought my son a car (eis or for) graduation. In other words: I bought my son a car (because of) graduation. I take medicine (eis or for) the pain. In other words: I take medicine (because of) the pain. He was unjustly crucified (eis or for) blasphemy. In other words: He was unjustly crucified (because of) blasphemy.

From these examples, it is easy to realize and understand that both words may be used in two totally different ways. It may be helpful if we ask ourselves the following simple questions: Do I take medicine (to receive) the pain? Or Do I take medicine (because of) the pain? It may be helpful to take a look at some verses which use the Greek preposition eis as "on the basis of," or "because of."

The first two verses we will look at are Mat. 12:41 and Luke 11:32.

The men of Nineveh will stand up at the judgment with this generation and condemn it; for they repented at the preaching of Jonah, and now one greater than Jonah is here.
— NIV, Mat. 12:41

The people of Nineveh will rise up at the judgment with this generation and condemn it, because they repented at the proclamation of Jonah, and see, something greater than Jonah is here!
— NRSV, Mat. 12:41

The men of Nineveh shall rise in judgment with this generation, and shall condemn it: because they repented {at} the preaching of Jonas; and, behold, a greater than Jonas is here.
— KJV, Mat. 12:41

The second verse which we will look at is Luke 11:32.

The men of Nineveh will stand up at the judgment with this generation and condemn it; for they repented at the preaching of Jonah, and now one greater than Jonah is here.
— NIV, Luke 11:32.

The people of Nineveh will rise up at the judgment with this generation and condemn it, because they repented at the proclamation of Jonah, and see, something greater than Jonah is here!
— NRSV, Luke 11:32

The men of Nineveh shall rise up in the judgment with this generation, and shall condemn it: for they repented {at} the preaching of Jonas; and, behold, a greater than Jonas is here.
— KJV, Luke 11:32

The word: "at" in both of these verses (Mat. 12:41 and Luke 11:32) is translated from the same Greek preposition eis, which is found in Acts 2:38: "for the remission of sins." Realizing that eis may be used two totally different ways, it may be helpful to ask ourselves a very simple question: Did the men of Niveveh repent in order to receive the preaching of Jonas? Or did the men of Niveveh repent because of the preaching of Jonas? I honestly believe that it would be nothing short of total foolishness for anyone to suggest or believe that the men of Nineveh repented to receive the preaching of Jonas. However, if total foolishness is a possibility here, then we have Scripture, which plainly informs us of the sequence of this historical event. First came the preaching by Jonah (Jonah 3:4). Then the men of Niveveh believed (Jonah 3:5). Then the men of Niveveh repented (Jonah 3:8). Then God's merciful grace was given (Jonah 3:10). The men of Niveveh repented: "Eis" – "at": because of the preaching of Jonas (Mat. 12:41 and Luke 11:32).

The third verse we will look at is Mat. 3:11.

"I baptize you with water for repentance. But after me will come one who is more powerful than I, whose sandals I am not fit to carry. He will baptize you with the Holy Spirit and with fire.
— *NIV, Mat. 3:11*

"I baptize you with water for repentance, but one who is more powerful than I is coming after me; I am not worthy to carry his sandals. He will baptize you with the Holy Spirit and fire.
— *NRSV, Mat. 3:11*

I indeed baptize you with water {unto} repentance: but he that cometh after me is mightier than I, whose shoes I am not worthy to bear: he shall baptize you with the Holy Ghost, and with fire
— *KJV, Mat. 3:11*

Once again, it may be helpful to simply ask ourselves a very simple question: Did John baptize people with water {eis — unto; to receive} repentance? Or did John baptize people with water {eis – unto; because of} repentance? The simplicity of this question should be apparent; if not, Scripture has graciously provided us with the answer.

[7] But when he saw many of the Pharisees and Sadducees come to his baptism, he said unto them, O generation of vipers, who hath warned you to flee from the wrath to come? [8] Bring forth therefore fruits meet for repentance:
— *(KJV) Mat. 3:7-8*

Repentance was necessary for an individual to be baptized by John the Baptist. The historical fact is that repentance was the requirement for an individual to be baptized by John the Baptist. This fact can never be argued or denied by anyone. Realizing that repentance was necessary for an individual to be baptized by John, we will now return to Mat. 3:11.

In Mat. 3:11, the word "unto" (KJV) is translated from the same Greek preposition eis, also found in Acts 2:38 "for the remission of sins." John's declaration in this verse (Mat. 3:11) is very valuable. The reason is that in both verses (Mat. 3:11 and Acts 2:38), the same verb "baptize" and the same Greek preposition "eis" are present. Also, in both verses the same verb "baptize" is modified by the same Greek preposition "eis." John's declaration, "I indeed baptize you with water unto repentance," means, "I indeed baptize you with water {unto – eis – for – because of} repentance."

The certainty and clarity of these facts are evident and are not dependent on the number of degrees an individual may or may not have. We must realize that God is not a God of confusion, nor is He a God of contradiction. Confusion and contradiction belong to man and are the result of man's limited abilities. God's total harmony of Scripture can never be heard perfectly by any individual. It is simply beyond man's ability. If we think of verses and view them as musical notes, we should realize that we must hear a harmonious melody. Our responsibility is to correctly hear as many spiritual notes as we possibly can. The beauty of any melody is dependent on its harmony. Acts 2:38, when read as a baptismal regeneration note, becomes a musical note without any Scriptural harmony. A flat and sour note placed in a melody of harmonious grace. To insist and believe that baptism is literally for the remission of sins would be, in my opinion, an act of total disregard for the vast majority of Scripture. If you presently believe in baptismal regeneration, you may be asking yourself: *How can he make a statement like that?* Please remember, I do not want you to take my word for it! I have spent many hours comparing baptismal regeneration theology to many verses. The result has always been the same; a flat and sour note lacking harmonious grace. The note I hear is not as important as the note you hear. You should compare and listen and then decide what kind of note you hear.

He who has ears, let him hear.

— *NIV, Mat. 11:15*

If we compare Acts 2:38 to a verse like Romans 10:10, there is absolutely no possibility of harmony at all, in my opinion.

149

Then Peter said unto them, Repent, and be baptized every one of you in the name of Jesus Christ {for} the remission of sins, and ye shall receive the gift of the Holy Ghost.

— KJV, Acts 2:38

For with the heart man believeth {unto} righteousness; and with the mouth confession is made {unto} salvation.

— KJV, Rom. 10:10

The same Greek preposition eis is used in both of these verses. If we understand "for" or "eis" in Acts 2:38 as "be baptized to receive the remission of sins," then when we compare this understanding and theology to Romans 10:10, there is no harmony and we are faced with a flat and sour note. However, if we understand "for" or "eis" in Acts 2:38 as "be baptized because of the remission of sins," then when we compare these two verses we hear total harmony full of grace!

The continuation of this controversy is nothing short of total silliness, in my opinion. We have numerous verses of Scripture which plainly place the remission of sins and spiritual life on the act of repentance (Mark 4:12, Acts 3:19, Acts 11:18, Rom. 10:10 and 2 Pet. 3:9). The continuation and attempted justification of this controversy are totally beyond my level of intelligence. However, in all honesty, we should remember that I have no formal degrees of education. My uneducated understanding of Scripture is that:

(1) we are converted by the act of repentance and our sins are blotted out:

Repent ye therefore, and be converted, that your sins may be blotted out, when the times of refreshing shall come from the presence of the Lord

— KJV, Acts 3:19

The entire third chapter of the Acts is dedicated to Peter's second recorded sermon. Baptism is never once mentioned in this chapter; however, we are informed that we are converted and that our sins are blotted out by repentance. It is also very important to realize the results of Peter's second recorded sermon: "But many who heard the message believed, and the number of men grew to about five thousand" (NIV, Acts 4:4). They heard, they believe, they repented and theirs sins were blotted out; this is God's merciful amazing complete grace (Acts 3:19).

(2) We are saved by the act of confession:

For with the heart man believeth unto righteousness; and with the mouth confession is made unto salvation.

— KJV, Rom. 10:10

(3) We are given spiritual life for the act of repentance:

When they heard these things, they held their peace, and glorified God, saying, Then hath God also to the Gentiles granted repentance unto life.

— KJV, Acts 11:18

(4) We will not perish if we repent:

The Lord is not slack concerning his promise, as some men count slackness; but is longsuffering to us-ward, not willing that any should perish, but that all should come to repentance.

— KJV, 2 Pet. 3:9

Any piece of the whole (Acts 2:38) is only a part of the whole. Any part of the whole (Acts 2:38) must conform to the whole. Any attempt to conform the whole to any given part of the whole (Acts 2:38) would be both destructive and unfair to the whole!

Please read that again and think about it.

Chapter 13

Conversion

CONVERT/ HEBREW WORD: SHUWB

Strong's Concordance:
H7725. shuwb, shoob; a prim. root; to turn back (hence, away) trans. or intrans., lit. or fig. (not necessarily with the idea of return to the starting point); gen. to retreat; often adv. again:— ([break, build, circumcise, dig, do anything, do evil, feed, lay down, lie down, lodge, make, rejoice, send, take, weep]) X again, (cause to) answer (+ again), X in any case (wise), X at all, averse, bring (again, back, home again), call [to mind], carry again (back), cease, X certainly, come again (back) X consider, + continually, convert, deliver (again), + deny, draw back, fetch home again, X fro, get [oneself] (back) again, X give (again), go again (back, home), [go] out, hinder, let, [see] more, X needs, be past, X pay, pervert, pull in again, put (again, up again), recall, recompense, recover, refresh, relieve, render (again), X repent, requite, rescue, restore, retrieve, (cause to, make to) return, reverse, reward, + say nay, send back, set again, slide back, still, X surely, take back (off), (cause to, make to) turn (again, self again, away, back, back again, backward, from, off), withdraw.

I believe that we should now allow ourselves to take a closer look at a word which has great meaning to every Christian. The word is convert or conversion. As we study the following section, I would like you to compare Acts 2:38 to the verses which we will be studying, and then ask yourself: *Do I hear harmony or do I hear a flat and sour note?* You decide what you hear. I have made my decision.

In the King James Version of the Bible, in the Old Testament we see the Hebrew word "shuwb," pronounced "shoob," translated as: convert, turn, repent, return, converted and restore.

The words in the following verses which have {brackets} are only a few examples of how the Hebrew word shuwb may be translated.

Therefore say unto the house of Israel, Thus saith the Lord GOD; {Repent}, and {turn} yourselves from your idols; and {turn} away your faces from all your abominations.

— *KJV, Ezek. 14:6*

But if the wicked will {turn} from all his sins that he hath committed, and keep all my statutes, and do that which is lawful and right, he shall surely live, he shall not die.

— *KJV, Ezek. 18:21*

[30] Therefore I will judge you, O house of Israel, every one according to his ways, saith the Lord GOD. {Repent}, and {turn} yourselves from all your transgressions; so iniquity shall not be your ruin. [31] Cast away from you all your transgressions, whereby ye have transgressed; and make you a new heart and a new spirit: for why will ye die, O house of Israel? [32] For I have no pleasure in the death of him that dieth, saith the Lord GOD: wherefore {turn} yourselves, and live ye.

— *KJV, Ezek. 18:30-32*

Make the heart of this people fat, and make their ears heavy, and shut their eyes; lest they see with their eyes, and hear with their ears, and understand with their heart, and {convert}, and be healed.

— *KJV, Isa. 6:10*

And he said, It is a light thing that thou shouldest be my servant to raise up the tribes of Jacob, and to {restore} the preserved of Israel: I will also give thee for a light to the Gentiles, that thou mayest be my salvation unto the end of the earth.

— *Isa. 49:6*

[12] {Restore} unto me the joy of thy salvation; and uphold me with thy free spirit. [13] Then will I teach transgressors thy ways; and sinners shall be {converted} unto thee.

— *KJV, Psa. 51:12-13*

{Turn} us again, O God, and cause thy face to shine; and we shall be saved.

— *KJV, Psa. 80:3*

Let those that fear thee {turn} unto me, and those that have known thy testimonies.

— *KJV, Psa. 119:79*

Yet if they shall bethink themselves in the land whither they were carried captives, and {repent}, and make supplication unto thee in the land of them that carried them captives, saying, We have sinned, and have done perversely, we have committed wickedness

— *KJV, 1 Ki. 8:47*

It is easy to realize from these verses that the Hebrew word "shuwb," means: convert, turn, repent, return, converted and restore. Convert means: to turn. To turn means: to convert. We are children of wrath by nature (Eph. 2:3), walking in spiritual darkness, being deceived by Satan, (Acts 26:18). God has send forth His Son: "I have come into the world as a light, so that no one who believes in me should stay in darkness" (NIV, John 12:46). If we turn to God, we are turning away from idols. When we turn to God, we are turning away from Satan, as we turn away from Satan we are turning away from sin. Turning away from Satan and sin and turning to God is only possible when faith is within us. Without faith, we would continue to serve the lusts of the flesh; the carnal mind would continue to control our thoughts and our actions. Our desires would be only to fulfill the lusts of our sinful mind and our sinful nature. Our desire to turn away from this way of life and to live a life, which glorifies Christ is nothing less than faith. We read about the Holy Spirit's role of conviction:

8 When he comes, he will convict the world of guilt in regard to sin and righteousness and judgment: 9 in regard to sin, because men do not believe in me

— NIV, John 16:8-9

The message of the gospel, the Holy Spirit and faith are the necessary spiritual elements for conviction and guilt. Faith, conviction and guilt lead us to repentance. Repentance is an act of our faith and the act of repentance is necessary for forgiveness (Ezek. 18:30-32). Forgiveness is restoration; a right relationship with God. Faith, which does not lead someone to a personal act of repentance, is not saving faith. Such faith is not a living faith and bears no fruit at all. Repentance is the first spiritual fruit produced by someone who has real faith. We must turn away from idols and false gods (Satan) before we can turn ourselves to God. It is impossible to turn away from Satan before we hear the written word of God, which has been given to mankind by God's grace. Repentance separates unconverted from converted and forgiven men.

The word conversion is found only once in the New Testament (Acts 15:3) in the King James Version. The Greek word from which "conversion" is translated from in this verse is "Epistrophe."

Strong's Concordance:
G1995. epistrophe, ep-is-trof-ay'; reversion, i.e. mor. revolution: —conversion, from G1994; epistrepho.

And being brought on their way by the church, they passed through Phenice and Samaria, declaring the conversion of the Gentiles: and they caused great joy unto all the brethren.

— KJV, Acts 15:3

155

Although the word conversion is only found once in the KJV, the words convert and converted are found more numerously and are translated from the Greek word "Epistrepho."

Strong's Concordance:
G1994. epistrepho, ep-ee-stref'-o; from G1909 and G4762; to revert (lit., fig. or mor.): —come (go) again, convert, (re-) turn (about, again).

The following verses are examples where Epistrepho is translated as "converted."

For this people's heart is waxed gross, and their ears are dull of hearing, and their eyes they have closed; lest at any time they should see with their eyes and hear with their ears, and should understand with their heart, and should be converted, and I should heal them.
— KJV, Mat. 13:15

That seeing they may see, and not perceive; and hearing they may hear, and not understand; lest at any time they should be converted, and their sins should be forgiven them.
— KJV, Mark 4:12

But I have prayed for thee, that thy faith fail not: and when thou art converted, strengthen thy brethren.
— KJV, Luke 22:32

He hath blinded their eyes, and hardened their heart; that they should not see with their eyes, nor understand with their heart, and be converted, and I should heal them.
— KJV, John 12:40

Repent ye therefore, and be converted, that your sins may be blotted out, when the times of refreshing shall come from the presence of the Lord;
— KJV, Acts 3:19

For the heart of this people is waxed gross, and their ears are dull of hearing, and their eyes have they closed; lest they should see with their eyes, and hear with their ears, and understand with their heart, and should be converted, and I should heal them.

— KJV, Acts 28:27

Another Greek word, "Strepho," is also translated as converted.

Strong's Concordance:
4762. strepho, stref'-o; strengthened from the base of G5157; to twist, i.e. turn quite around or reverse (lit. or fig.):—convert, turn (again, back again, self, self about).

The following verse is an example:

And said, Verily I say unto you, Except ye be converted, and become as little children, ye shall not enter into the kingdom of heaven.

— KJV, Mat. 18:3

Epistrepho is also translated as convert and converteth.

[19] Brethren, if any of you do err from the truth, and one convert him; [20] Let him know, that he which converteth the sinner from the error of his way shall save a soul from death, and shall hide a multitude of sins.

— KJV, James 5:19-20

The same Greek word, epistrepho, translated as converted, convert and converteth is also translated as "turn" and "turned." The following are only a few of many examples.

And saying, Sirs, why do ye these things? We also are men of like passions with you, and preach unto you that ye should turn from these vanities unto the living God, which made heaven, and earth, and the sea, and all things that are therein

— KJV, Acts 14:15

To open their eyes, and to turn them from darkness to light, and from the power of Satan unto God, that they may receive forgiveness of sins, and inheritance among them which are sanctified by faith that is in me.

— *KJV, Acts 26:18*

But showed first unto them of Damascus, and at Jerusalem, and throughout all the coasts of Judaea, and then to the Gentiles, that they should repent and turn to God, and do works meet for repentance.

— *KJV, Acts 26:20*

For they themselves show of us what manner of entering in we had unto you, and how ye turned to God from idols to serve the living and true God

— *KJV, 1 Th. 1:9*

The act of repentance is a spiritual act, which demonstrates our personal faith and trust. Repentance is conversion.

That seeing they may see, and not perceive; and hearing they may hear, and not understand; lest at any time they should be converted, and their sins should be forgiven them.

— *KJV, Mark 4:12*

In the third chapter of the Book of Acts, Peter is preaching his second recorded sermon (Acts 3:12-3:26).

Repent ye therefore, and be converted, that your sins may be blotted out, when the times of refreshing shall come from the presence of the Lord

— *KJV, Acts 3:19*

These verses (Acts 3:19 & Mark 4:12) are so wonderful and should be to us more precious and more valuable than gold. The words recorded in these verses are not the words of men. They are the inspired written words of God. We are informed in Acts 3:19 "Repent ye therefore, and be converted, that your sins may be blotted out, when the times of refreshing shall come from the presence of the Lord." By the act of repentance, we are converted and our sins are blotted out. We are also informed by the inspired written words of Jesus in Mark 4:12, "That seeing they may see, and not perceive; and hearing they may hear, and not understand; lest at any time they should be converted, and their sins should be forgiven them." From these two verses (Acts 3:19 & Mark 4:12) we should easily realize that we are converted by repentance (Acts 3:19) and our sins are forgiven when we are converted.

In the first few verses in the fourth chapter of Acts, we see the dual result of Peter's second recorded sermon (Acts 3:12-3:26).

¹ The priests and the captain of the temple guard and the Sadducees came up to Peter and John while they were speaking to the people. ² They were greatly disturbed because the apostles were teaching the people and proclaiming in Jesus the resurrection of the dead. ³ They seized Peter and John, and because it was evening, they put them in jail until the next day.
— NIV, Acts 4:1-3

"The priests and the captain of the temple guard and the Sadducees ... seized Peter and John ... and put them in jail." Peter's second sermon was preached a short time, perhaps even within days, after his first sermon, which had been preached by him on the Day of Pentecost. Peter never once mentions baptism in his second recorded sermon (Acts 3:12 -3:26). However, "the number of men grew to about five thousand."

But many who heard the message believed, and the number of men grew to about five thousand. ›
— NIV, Acts 4:4

The message heard and believed was, "Repent ye therefore, and be converted, that your sins may be blotted out, when the times of refreshing shall come from the presence of the Lord" (Acts 3:19). Converted and forgiven by repentance: God's Amazing Grace! These two beautiful verses (Acts 3:19 & Mark 4:12) really illustrate the simplicity of conversion. We turn away from Satan and we turn to God, because we have faith, we repent; and we are converted by repenting and our sins are forgiven.

I tell you, Nay: but, except ye repent, ye shall all likewise perish.
— KJV, Luke 13:3

When we repent, we humble ourselves like little children before God.

³ And said, Verily I say unto you, Except ye be converted, and become as little children, ye shall not enter into the kingdom of heaven. ⁴ Whosoever therefore shall humble himself as this little child, the same is greatest in the kingdom of heaven.
— KJV, Mat. 18:3

We are converted by our personal act of repentance and our sins are blotted out. In the following parable, Jesus also informs us that we are justified when we acknowledge and confess ours sins.

¹⁰ "Two men went up to the temple to pray, one a Pharisee and the other a tax collector. ¹¹ The Pharisee stood up and prayed about himself: 'God, I thank you that I am not like other men—robbers, evildoers, adulterers—or even like this tax collector. ¹² I fast twice a week and give a tenth of all I get.' ¹³ But the tax collector stood at a distance. He would not even look up to heaven, but beat his breast and said, 'God, have mercy on me, a sinner.' ¹⁴ I tell you that this man, rather than the other, went home justified before God. For everyone who exalts himself will be humbled, and he who humbles himself will be exalted."
— NIV, Luke 18:10-14.

"God, have mercy on me, a sinner ... I tell you that this man ... went home justified before God"(18:14). Repentance is conversion. Repentance is not only an act of faith; repentance is also an act of acknowledgment. When we repent, we are not only demonstrating our faith in and to a merciful God; we are also acknowledging that we are guilty shameful sinners to a gracious merciful forgiving God. By God's merciful grace, forgiveness is given for repentance. The Apostle Paul also informs us of the same thing.

[8] But what saith it? The word is nigh thee, even in thy mouth, and in thy heart: that is, the word of faith, which we preach; [9] That if thou shalt confess with thy mouth the Lord Jesus, and shalt believe in thine heart that God hath raised him from the dead, thou shalt be saved. [10] For with the heart man believeth unto righteousness; and with the mouth confession is made unto salvation.

— KJV, Rom. 10:8-10

"That if thou shalt confess with thy mouth the Lord Jesus and believe that God hath raised him from the dead thou shalt be saved. For with the mouth confession is made unto salvation."

In Hebrew, "shuwb" (Ezek. 14:6 and Ezek. 18:30-32), and also in Greek, "epistrepho" (Mark 4:12 and Acts 3:19), convert means: to turn. To turn means: to convert. God's grace gives forgiveness of sins for repentance. By God's merciful grace, atonement has already been made for the sins of all mankind. The sacrificial lamb, which provided this atonement for me and for you was called by John the Baptist: "the Lamb of God" (John 1:29) who takes away the sin of the world!

[25] God presented him as a sacrifice of atonement, through faith in his blood. He did this to demonstrate his justice, because in his forbearance he had left the sins committed beforehand unpunished— [26] he did it to demonstrate his justice at the present time, so as to be just and the one who justifies those who have faith in Jesus. [27] Where, then, is boasting? It is excluded. On what

161

principle? On that of observing the law? No, but on that of faith.
[28] For we maintain that a man is justified by faith apart from observing the law

— *NIV, Romans 3:25-28:*

In whom we have redemption through his blood, the forgiveness of sins, according to the riches of his grace

— *KJV, Eph. 1:7*

The spiritual light, which we receive from God's written word, informs us that God presented Jesus as a sacrifice of atonement. "Presented ... a sacrifice of atonement." How? By or "through faith in his blood." Faith in His blood for what? For the forgiveness or remission of sins. God's sacrificial lamb, which lived among us and who allowed himself to be nailed to a cross/altar, almost two thousand years ago said: "This is my blood of the covenant, which is poured out for many for the forgiveness of sins" (NIV, Mat. 26:28). The cost of man's redemption was great. "For you know that it was not with perishable things such as silver or gold that you were redeemed from the empty way of life handed down to you from your forefathers, but with the precious blood of Christ, a lamb without blemish or defect" (NIV, 1 Peter 1:18-19).

The atonement has been made. Christ crucified. The blood has been shed for the remission of sins. The ransom has been paid. The only thing which stands between atonement and redemption is our faith in His blood for the forgiveness or remission of sins (Romans 3:25 and Eph. 1:7) and our personal act of repentance for the forgiveness of sins (Mark 4:12, Acts 3:19). By God's merciful grace, forgiveness is given for repentance. Conversion is forgiveness of sins by God's grace through repentance.

And that repentance and remission of sins should be preached in his name among all nations, beginning at Jerusalem.

— *KJV, Luke 24:47*

In the past God overlooked such ignorance, but now he commands all people everywhere to repent.

— *NIV, Acts 17:30*

Convert: to turn to God. Repent: converted. Conversion: converted by repentance. An example of the importance of repentance: After David had arranged for Bathsheba's husband to go to battle, where he was killed, King David committed adultery with Bathsheba. God used the prophet Nathan to rebuke King David (2 Samuel 12:7-9). David humbled himself and acknowledged his sins and repented before God in prayer. David's heartfelt and sincere prayer of repentance is recorded in Psalm 51:1-19. David's prayer of sincere repentance is an example of the attitude and sincerity we should have when we repent and seek God's gracious merciful forgiveness.

"I baptize you with water for repentance. But after me will come one who is more powerful than I, whose sandals I am not fit to carry. He will baptize you with the Holy Spirit and with fire."
— NIV, Mat. 3:11

John did baptize in the wilderness, and preach the baptism of repentance for the remission of sins.
— KJV, Mark 1:4

I would like you to ask yourself: *Did John baptize people so that they would then repent after they had been baptized? Or did John baptize people who had already repented?* John only baptized people who had already repented for the remission of their sins (Mat. 3:8 & Mat. 3:11). They repented because they believed. They were baptized because they had repented for the remission of sins (Mark 1:4). Baptism was only a sign of their act of repentance. Baptism symbolized their faith and their repentance.

And they went out, and preached that men should repent.
— KJV, Mark 6:12

Repent ye therefore, and be converted, that your sins may be blotted out, when the times of refreshing shall come from the presence of the Lord
— KJV, Acts 3:19

God exalted him to his own right hand as Prince and Savior that he might give repentance and forgiveness of sins to Israel.

— *NIV, Acts 5:31*

When they heard these things, they held their peace, and glorified God, saying, Then hath God also to the Gentiles granted repentance unto life.

— *KJV, Acts 11:18*

And the times of this ignorance God winked at; but now commandeth all men every where to repent.

— *KJV, Acts 17:30*

9 That if you confess with your mouth, "Jesus is Lord," and believe in your heart that God raised him from the dead, you will be saved. 10 For it is with your heart that you believe and are justified, and it is with your mouth that you confess and are saved. 11 As the Scripture says, "Anyone who trusts in him will never be put to shame." 12 For there is no difference between Jew and Gentile—the same Lord is Lord of all and richly blesses all who call on him, 13 for, "Everyone who calls on the name of the Lord will be saved."

— *NIV, Rom. 10:9-13*

The Lord is not slow in keeping his promise, as some understand slowness. He is patient with you, not wanting anyone to perish, but everyone to come to repentance.

— *NIV, 2 Pet. 3:9*

The spiritual light, which we are given in the above verses, informs us that God exalted him to his own right hand as Prince and Savior that he might give repentance and forgiveness of sins to Israel (NIV, Acts 5:31). "For there is no difference between Jew and Gentile—the same Lord is Lord of all and richly blesses all who call on him, for, Everyone who calls on the name of the Lord will be saved."(NIV, Rom. 10:12-13). The Lord is not slow in keeping his promise, as some understand slowness. "He is patient with you, not wanting anyone to perish, but everyone to come to repentance" (NIV, 2 Pet. 3:9). "Repent ye therefore, and be converted, that your sins may be blotted out, when the times of refreshing shall come from the presence of the Lord" (KJV, Acts 3:19).

From the above study of conversion, repentance and forgiveness, I would like to encourage you to ask yourself the following questions.

1. How and when does God forgive sins?
2. How are we converted?
3. What note do I now hear in Acts 2:38 an (eis - to receive) note or an (eis - because of) note?

Pieces of the whole conforming to the whole!

Chapter 14

One Lord, One Faith, One Baptism

Let's attempt now to put it all together with nothing but Scripture. This has been my goal from the beginning. The spiritual sword of the Holy Spirit is more powerful than any words which could ever be spoken or written by me or any other man.

¹⁶ I am not ashamed of the gospel, because it is the power of God for the salvation of everyone who believes: first for the Jew, then for the Gentile. ¹⁷ For in the gospel a righteousness from God is revealed, a righteousness that is by faith from first to last, just as it is written: "The righteous will live by faith."

— NIV, Rom. 1:16-17

What does the Scripture say? "Abraham believed God, and it was credited to him as righteousness."

— NIV, Rom. 4:3

¹⁷ As it is written: "I have made you a father of many nations." He is our father in the sight of God, in whom he believed—the God who gives life to the dead and calls things that are not as though they were. ¹⁸ Against all hope, Abraham in hope believed and so became the father of many nations, just as it had been said to him, "So shall your offspring be." ¹⁹ Without weakening in his faith, he faced the fact that his body was as good as dead—since he was

about a hundred years old—and that Sarah's womb was also dead. [20] Yet he did not waver through unbelief regarding the promise of God, but was strengthened in his faith and gave glory to God, [21] being fully persuaded that God had power to do what he had promised. [22] This is why it was credited to him as righteousness. [23] The words it was credited to him were written not for him alone, [24] but also for us, to whom God will credit righteousness—for us who believe in him who raised Jesus our Lord from the dead. [25] He was delivered over to death for our sins and was raised to life for our justification.

— *NIV, Rom. 4:17-25*

[8] *Blessed is the man whose sin the Lord will never count against him." [9] Is this blessedness only for the circumcised, or also for the uncircumcised? We have been saying that Abraham's faith was credited to him as righteousness. [10] Under what circumstances was it credited? Was it after he was circumcised, or before? It was not after, but before! [11] And he received the sign of circumcision, a seal of the righteousness that he had by faith while he was still uncircumcised. So then, he is the father of all who believe but have not been circumcised, in order that righteousness might be credited to them. [12] And he is also the father of the circumcised who not only are circumcised but who also walk in the footsteps of the faith that our father Abraham had before he was circumcised. [13] It was not through law that Abraham and his offspring received the promise that he would be heir of the world, but through the righteousness that comes by faith. [14] For if those who live by law are heirs, faith has no value and the promise is worthless,*

— *NIV, Rom. 4:8-14*

Therefore, the promise comes by faith, so that it may be by grace and may be guaranteed to all Abraham's offspring—not only to those who are of the law but also to those who are of the faith of Abraham. He is the father of us all.

— *NIV, Rom. 4:16*

Now the first covenant had regulations for worship and also an earthly sanctuary.
— NIV, Heb. 9:1

[8] The Holy Spirit was showing by this that the way into the Most Holy Place had not yet been disclosed as long as the first tabernacle was still standing. [9] This is an illustration for the present time, indicating that the gifts and sacrifices being offered were not able to clear the conscience of the worshiper. [10] They are only a matter of food and drink and various ceremonial washings—external regulations applying until the time of the new order. [11] When Christ came as high priest of the good things that are already here, he went through the greater and more perfect tabernacle that is not man-made, that is to say, not a part of this creation. [12] He did not enter by means of the blood of goats and calves; but he entered the Most Holy Place once for all by his own blood, having obtained eternal redemption. [13] The blood of goats and bulls and the ashes of a heifer sprinkled on those who are ceremonially unclean sanctify them so that they are outwardly clean. [14] How much more, then, will the blood of Christ, who through the eternal Spirit offered himself unblemished to God, cleanse our consciences from acts that lead to death, so that we may serve the living God! [15] For this reason Christ is the mediator of a new covenant, that those who are called may receive the promised eternal inheritance—now that he has died as a ransom to set them free from the sins committed under the first covenant.
— NIV, Heb. 9:8-15

Therefore, when Christ came into the world, he said: "Sacrifice and offering you did not desire, but a body you prepared for me;
— NIV, Heb. 10:5

Then he said, "Here I am, I have come to do your will." He sets aside the first to establish the second.
— NIV, Heb. 10:9

This is my blood of the covenant, which is poured out for many for the forgiveness of sins.

— NIV, Mat. 26:28

[50] *And when Jesus had cried out again in a loud voice, he gave up his spirit.* [51] *At that moment the curtain of the temple was torn in two from top to bottom. The earth shook and the rocks split.*

— NIV, Mat. 27:50-51

Therefore, just as sin entered the world through one man, and death through sin, and in this way death came to all men, because all sinned

— NIV, Rom. 5:12

Consequently, just as the result of one trespass was condemnation for all men, so also the result of one act of righteousness was justification that brings life for all men.

— NIV, Rom. 5:18

[11] *Clearly no one is justified before God by the law, because, "The righteous will live by faith."* [12] *The law is not based on faith; on the contrary, "The man who does these things will live by them."* [13] *Christ redeemed us from the curse of the law by becoming a curse for us, for it is written: "Cursed is everyone who is hung on a tree."* [14] *He redeemed us in order that the blessing given to Abraham might come to the Gentiles through Christ Jesus, so that by faith we might receive the promise of the Spirit.*

— NIV, Gal. 3:11-14

So the law was put in charge to lead us to Christ that we might be justified by faith.

— NIV, Gal. 3:24

[8] *For it is by grace you have been saved, through faith—and this not from yourselves, it is the gift of God—* [9] *not by works, so that no one can boast.*

— NIV, Eph. 2:8-9

[12] For there is no difference between Jew and Gentile—the same Lord is Lord of all and richly blesses all who call on him, [13] for, "Everyone who calls on the name of the Lord will be saved." [14] How, then, can they call on the one they have not believed in? And how can they believe in the one of whom they have not heard? And how can they hear without someone preaching to them?

— NIV, Rom. 10:12-14

[13] When you were dead in your sins and in the uncircumcision of your sinful nature, God made you alive with Christ. He forgave us all our sins, [14] having canceled the written code, with its regulations, that was against us and that stood opposed to us; he took it away, nailing it to the cross.

— NIV, Col. 2:13-14

[17] For Christ did not send me to baptize, but to preach the gospel— not with words of human wisdom, lest the cross of Christ be emptied of its power. [18] For the message of the cross is foolishness to those who are perishing, but to us who are being saved it is the power of God. [19] For it is written: "I will destroy the wisdom of the wise; the intelligence of the intelligent I will frustrate." [20] Where is the wise man? Where is the scholar? Where is the philosopher of this age? Has not God made foolish the wisdom of the world? [21] For since in the wisdom of God the world through its wisdom did not know him, God was pleased through the foolishness of what was preached to save those who believe. [22] Jews demand miraculous signs and Greeks look for wisdom, [23] but we preach Christ crucified: a stumbling block to Jews and foolishness to Gentiles, [24] but to those whom God has called, both Jews and Greeks, Christ the power of God and the wisdom of God. [25] For the foolishness of God is wiser than man's wisdom, and the weakness of God is stronger than man's strength.

— NIV, 1Cor. 1:17-25

[1] Now, brothers, I want to remind you of the gospel I preached to you, which you received and on which you have taken your

stand. [2] By this gospel you are saved, if you hold firmly to the word I preached to you. Otherwise, you have believed in vain. [3] For what I received I passed on to you as of first importance: that Christ died for our sins according to the Scriptures, [4] that he was buried, that he was raised on the third day according to the Scriptures,

— NIV, 1Cor. 15:1-4

In him we have redemption through his blood, the forgiveness of sins, in accordance with the riches of God's grace.

— NIV, Eph. 1:7

[21] But now a righteousness from God, apart from law, has been made known, to which the Law and the Prophets testify. [22] This righteousness from God comes through faith in Jesus Christ to all who believe. There is no difference, [23] for all have sinned and fall short of the glory of God, [24] and are justified freely by his grace through the redemption that came by Christ Jesus.

— NIV, Rom. 3:21-24

[27] Where, then, is boasting? It is excluded. On what principle? On that of observing the law? No, but on that of faith. [28] For we maintain that a man is justified by faith apart from observing the law.

— NIV, Rom. 3:27-28

[25] God presented him as a sacrifice of atonement, through faith in his blood. He did this to demonstrate his justice, because in his forbearance he had left the sins committed beforehand unpunished— [26] he did it to demonstrate his justice at the present time, so as to be just and the one who justifies those who have faith in Jesus.

— NIV, Rom. 3:25-26

[9] Since we have now been justified by his blood, how much more shall we be saved from God's wrath through him! [10] For if, when

we were God's enemies, we were reconciled to him through the death of his Son, how much more, having been reconciled, shall we be saved through his life!

— NIV, Rom. 5:9-10

God exalted him to his own right hand as Prince and Savior that he might give repentance and forgiveness of sins to Israel.

— NIV, Acts 5:31

[19] Therefore, brothers, since we have confidence to enter the Most Holy Place by the blood of Jesus, [20] by a new and living way opened for us through the curtain, that is, his body, [21] and since we have a great priest over the house of God, [22] let us draw near to God with a sincere heart in full assurance of faith, having our hearts sprinkled to cleanse us from a guilty conscience and having our bodies washed with pure water.

— NIV, Heb. 10:19-22

in whom we have redemption, the forgiveness of sins.

— NIV, Col. 1:14

In him and through faith in him we may approach God with freedom and confidence.

— NIV, Eph. 3:12

[4] Christ is the end of the law so that there may be righteousness for everyone who believes. [5] Moses describes in this way the righteousness that is by the law: "The man who does these things will live by them." [6] But the righteousness that is by faith says: "Do not say in your heart, 'Who will ascend into heaven?' " (that is, to bring Christ down) [7] "or 'Who will descend into the deep?' " (that is, to bring Christ up from the dead). [8] But what does it say? "The word is near you; it is in your mouth and in your heart," that is, the word of faith we are proclaiming: [9] That if you confess with your mouth, "Jesus is Lord," and believe in your heart that God raised him from the dead, you will be saved. [10] For it is with your

heart that you believe and are justified, and it is with your mouth that you confess and are saved.

— *NIV, Rom. 10:4-10*

[28] *A man is not a Jew if he is only one outwardly, nor is circumcision merely outward and physical.* [29] *No, a man is a Jew if he is one inwardly; and circumcision is circumcision of the heart, by the Spirit, not by the written code. Such a man's praise is not from men, but from God.*

— *NIV, Rom. 2:28-29*

For the word of God is living and active. Sharper than any double-edged sword, it penetrates even to dividing soul and spirit, joints and marrow; it judges the thoughts and attitudes of the heart.

— *NIV, Heb. 4:12*

[13] *And you also were included in Christ when you heard the word of truth, the gospel of your salvation. Having believed, you were marked in him with a seal, the promised Holy Spirit,* [14] *who is a deposit guaranteeing our inheritance until the redemption of those who are God's possession—to the praise of his glory.*

— *NIV, Eph. 1:13-14*

[4] *But because of his great love for us, God, who is rich in mercy,* [5] *made us alive with Christ even when we were dead in transgressions—it is by grace you have been saved.* [6] *And God raised us up with Christ and seated us with him in the heavenly realms in Christ Jesus,* [7] *in order that in the coming ages he might show the incomparable riches of his grace, expressed in his kindness to us in Christ Jesus.*

— *NIV, Eph. 2:4-7*

Godly sorrow brings repentance that leads to salvation and leaves no regret, but worldly sorrow brings death.

— *NIV, 2Cor. 7:10*

Repent ye therefore, and be converted, that your sins may be blotted out, when the times of refreshing shall come from the presence of the Lord;

— *KJV, Acts 3:19*

The Spirit himself testifies with our spirit that we are God's children.

— *NIV, Rom. 8:16*

The Lord is not slow in keeping his promise, as some understand slowness. He is patient with you, not wanting anyone to perish, but everyone to come to repentance.

— *NIV, 2 Pet. 3:9*

For we were all baptized by one Spirit into one body—whether Jews or Greeks, slave or free—and we were all given the one Spirit to drink.

— *NIV, 1Cor. 12:13*

There is one body and one Spirit— just as you were called to one hope when you were called

— *NIV, Eph. 4:4*

one Lord, one faith, one baptism;

— *NIV, Eph. 4:5*

I have shared with you a few things about myself. You already know that I never finished high school. You know that I am a steel worker. I would now like to share with you something which is very personal and painful for me. The sole purpose for writing this book is that I truly believe that my present understanding of Scripture is correct. As Christians, we have the responsibility of discernment and to defend the true Gospel of Jesus Christ. My desire to fulfill this responsibility is my sole reason for writing this book. If I had any uncertainty of this being true, I would never have written this book.

This book is dedicated to a person who will always be very dear and precious to me. A person who will forever be in my heart. This person is my son Rob. On the twenty-sixth of November, 1974, a gift from God was born and graciously given to my then-wife and myself. The eighteenth of June 1997 was a day my son and his friends had made plans for jet-skiing and fun. My son had no idea that his plans would never come to be a reality. While my son was waiting for his friends, someone cut the screen on the patio door and entered the house.

From what I have been told, the theory is one or two intruders entered the house. Apparently my son heard some noise, started walking down the staircase, and halfway down the intruder shot and his target was not hit. It appears that my son ran up the staircase into a bedroom, got a gun, and then returned to the staircase. Halfway down the staircase, many shots were exchanged and the life of my precious son was suddenly taken away.

I am totally unable to describe the pain a parent feels after the death of a child. I believe this to be true for most, if not all, individuals. I personally feel the same way when I think of God's amazing grace. I personally feel that words are incapable of describing God's complete grace.

I have decided to share this tragic story with you for a reason. The reason is my desire to share with you a story of God's grace and a story of hope which came from His amazing grace. For many years, my son had been in trouble and had been doing many things which he should not have been doing. For many years, my greatest fear had been that somewhere a bullet with my son's name on it was waiting for him if he chose not to change his way of life. I had shared this fear many times with Rob and also with many other people. Looking back, I am unable to explain why I had this fear, but I had lived with it for many years.

My present wife, Cindy, and I had been praying for two years that God would provide an opportunity for someone, anyone, to witness to Rob and for him to come to know Jesus as his Lord and Savior. We had not heard from Rob for several months. Then one night, a collect call from Rob brought joy and hope to our hearts. Rob was in a county jail somewhere in the state of Tennessee; I am honestly unable to remember the reason for his confinement. You may be asking yourself, *why did this bring joy and hope?* Cindy and I both believed and had hope in our hearts that our prayers had been answered. You see, Rob informed me that a man in jail would not leave him alone. This man was armed, in his hands lay a Bible and he was continuously witnessing to my son. This Christian man had told my son that God had told him that Rob was special and he was only to witness to Rob.

When Rob told me this, I almost fell out of my chair. I shared with my son that Cindy and I had been praying for this to happen for two years. I began to witness to Rob and my son told me that he realized that he had done many bad things and he believed that his confinement in jail was a punishment from God. My son told me that he was going to change his ways and start doing things right when he was released from jail. I told my son to continue to listen to this Christian man and to tell him that he was an answer to our prayers. I pleaded with my son that he needed to accept Jesus as his Savior. I told Rob that many times in life we are given only one opportunity to do some things. I told my son that I loved him, I said goodbye, never realizing that I would never see him again. Three months later, my son was dead. Oh, how I wish that I could hold my precious son in my arms again. I only pray that he is in the arms of his Lord and Savior.

When I received the call that my son was dead, I was studying the Book of Acts. I had just recently read Acts 11:26 which informs us that the disciples were called Christians first in Antioch. My son was shot and his life came to a sudden end in Antioch, Tennessee. Coincidence, maybe, and then again, maybe not. Whether my son was a Christian at the time of his death is known only by God.

What I do know is that God gives us strength when we feel there is no possible way to continue on our own strength. The strength we receive from God, is only possible because of God's grace. The hope, which many of us may have, is also possible only by His grace. Had I not received that phone call from my son, I would not have the hope of the possibility that maybe one day my precious son will be held in my arms once again. When I think back to this time in my life, I see in my mind only one set of footprints walking in the sand. I truly believe with all of my heart that God has provided me with hope and has also carried me during my greatest time of weakness. A time in my life which I believe would have been a moment in time when I would have been unable to continue to walk on my own strength alone.

I truly believe that there are many individuals who, like myself, have lost a loved one knowing that they were never baptized. If God requires baptism for forgiveness and salvation, then these individuals have no hope for the love ones they have lost. The unpleasant image in our mind of our loved ones being in Hell for eternity is then a true reality. Regardless of how unpleasant this image may be, it would still be an avoidable true reality for all mankind.

However, if baptism is not a requirement for salvation, then there is always the possibility that when our loved ones were facing the fear of death, they may have believed and repented before their deaths. This possibility then provides hope. Hope that our loved ones may have been saved and hope of being reunited with them on a future glorious day. Hope that provides strength; hope possible only by His amazing grace.

I praise God for His amazing grace and for the hope and strength He provides for our deepest needs in our greatest times of weakness.

Chapter 15

Baptism: What Is It?

My present understanding of Scripture is that Christian baptism is portrayed as something spiritual. Paul's symbolic uses of baptism are as follows:

³ Know ye not, that so many of us as were baptized into Jesus Christ were baptized into his death? ⁴ Therefore we are buried with him by baptism into death: that like as Christ was raised up from the dead by the glory of the Father, even so we also should walk in newness of life. ⁵ For if we have been planted together in the likeness of his death, we shall be also in the likeness of his resurrection: ⁶ Knowing this, that our old man is crucified with him, that the body of sin might be destroyed, that henceforth we should not serve sin. ⁷ For he that is dead is freed from sin. ⁸ Now if we be dead with Christ, we believe that we shall also live with him
— KJV, Rom. 6:3-8

From these few verses, it is easy to realize that Paul presents water baptism as a symbol or as a physical sign, which represents four different spiritual things for Christians. (1) Baptism symbolizes our spiritual crucifixion with Christ: "that our old man is crucified with him." (2) Baptism symbolizes our spiritual death: "in the likeness of his death" and "we be dead with Christ." (3) Baptism symbolizes our spiritual burial: "we are buried with him by baptism." (4) Baptism symbolizes our spiritual resurrection: "so we also should walk in newness of life."

We were not physically crucified. We did not physically die. We were not physically buried with Him and we were not physically resurrected. Spiritual crucifixion, spiritual death, spiritual burial and spiritual resurrection all occur before water baptism. When we hear the message of the gospel, the Holy Spirit is able to convict us of sin. We turn away from Satan and we turn to God. When we fall on our knees in confession and repentance, we are demonstrating our faith and trust in God. We are also demonstrating to God our desire to walk in newness of life. We have changed the way we think, the old man is being renewed in his mind, our old sinful ways are now disgusting to us. We have a new heart, full of faith, which now has new desires and new goals.

We spiritually crucify the old man and we spiritually die to the old man and his disgusting sinful ways. We spiritually bury the old man and we set our eyes and heart on Christ. With a pledge of alliance to God and a desire to walk in newness of life, we are spiritually resurrected. Our new desires are to serve God and to glorify nobody, except Jesus. This is why personal repentance is so important. This is why Paul preached that people should repent (Acts 26:20). This is why Paul wrote to the Christians in Rome and to us, "For with the heart man believeth unto righteousness; and with the mouth confession is made unto salvation" (KJV, Rom. 10:10). This is also why God has commanded all people everywhere to repent (Acts 17:30). Realizing that it is "with the mouth confession is made unto salvation" and also realizing that it is God's will and desire for all people to repent, we SHOULD be asking ourselves the following question: Why does God want all people to come to repentance(2 Pet. 3:9)?

That seeing they may see, and not perceive; and hearing they may hear, and not understand; lest at any time they should be converted, and their sins should be forgiven them.
— KJV, Mark 4:12

Repent ye therefore, and be converted, that your sins may be blotted out, when the times of refreshing shall come from the presence of the Lord
— KJV, Acts 3:19

When they heard these things, they held their peace, and glorified God, saying, Then hath God also to the Gentiles granted repentance unto life.

— KJV, Acts 11:18

For with the heart man believeth unto righteousness; and with the mouth confession is made unto salvation.

— KJV, Rom. 10:10

The Lord is not slack concerning his promise, as some men count slackness; but is longsuffering to us-ward, not willing that any should perish, but that all should come to repentance.

— KJV, 2 Pet. 3:9

We realize from the above verses and from our previous studies that spiritual life is given for repentance. We also see that repentance is conversion and forgiveness of sins. We should also realize that forgiveness of sins and salvation are both dependent on the act of repentance and not dependent on baptism. Forgiveness of sins and spiritual life are given for repentance (Mark 4:12, Acts 3:19, Acts 11:18, Rom. 10:10 & 2 Pet. 3:9). Let's assume for a moment that someone believes in baptismal regeneration.

We will attempt to look at forgiveness at a different angle, using Scripture as our guide. The following verses are instructions for all Christians:

[1] Be imitators of God, therefore, as dearly loved children [2] and live a life of love, just as Christ loved us and gave himself up for us as a fragrant offering and sacrifice to God.

— NIV, Eph. 5:1-2

[12] Therefore, as God's chosen people, holy and dearly loved, clothe yourselves with compassion, kindness, humility, gentleness and patience. [13] Bear with each other and forgive whatever grievances you may have against one another. Forgive as the Lord forgave you.

— NIV, Col. 3:12-13

³ *So watch yourselves. "If your brother sins, rebuke him, and if he repents, forgive him. ⁴ If he sins against you seven times in a day, and seven times comes back to you and says, 'I repent,' forgive him."*

— *NIV, Luke 17:3-4*

These verses give us spiritual light and also instruct us to be imitators of God, clothing ourselves with compassion, kindness, humility, gentleness and patience; we are also instructed to forgive one another. We have learned from our study that God graciously requires mankind to repent for forgiveness. God has then made forgiveness to us conditional. God also requires His children to forgive for repentance. God's amazing grace, forgiveness for repentance, which He has given and shown to us, is the same grace Christians are instructed to give and show to others. "be imitators of God"(Eph. 5:1). "So watch yourselves. If your brother sins, rebuke him, and if he repents, forgive him"(Luke 17:3). "Forgive as the Lord forgave you"(Col. 3:13). "If he repents" we are instructed to "forgive him." It is very easy for us to see that if baptism was literally for the forgiveness of sins, then Christians would be unable to "Forgive as the Lord forgave you"(Col. 3:13). The grace, which has been given, is the same grace we are instructed to give. Once again, pieces of the whole conforming to the whole.

We have studied numerous verses of Scripture, which plainly place forgiveness with repentance. In my opinion, to insist that an individual must be literally baptized for the remission of sins would be an act of distortion. Distortion of Scripture and also distortion of God's complete grace. The theology of baptismal regeneration requires the works of Christ on the cross plus the works of man. Water baptism is a physical act performed by an individual. Their goal for doing this is to attain the remission of sins for the individual whom they are baptizing. When an individual is literally baptized "for"- (to receive) the remission of sins, baptism becomes an act or work of man and also a ritual sacrament conveying God's grace of forgiveness. The individual who is being baptized is deliberately doing a physical act and their goal for doing this is to attain or receive the remission of their sins.

Something done by man, something done to man and something done for a desired goal of man.

Just as it is impossible to mix oil with water, it is also impossible to mix grace with merit. Any amount of merit, being baptized for – to receive, the remission of sins eliminates grace. Grace can only remain grace when nothing is added. Physical works of any kind, regardless of how righteous they may be, gives birth to merit. Being baptized for – to receive the remission of sins is a deliberate physical act: Something done by man, something done for man. Any amount of merit and grace is no longer grace. Merit and grace truly are like oil and water: Totally impossible to mix and remain the same.

If this is not a physical work of man in your opinion, then I would like to ask you: What is? The completeness of our atonement and redemption were totally achieved by Christ. Nothing was left unfinished, nothing was left dependent on anyone else, for in Christ, is all our needs. I honestly believe that we must try to view and understand Scripture as a whole. We should never try to conform the whole to any piece of the whole. We must always try to conform any given piece of the whole (Acts 2:38) to the whole. I realize that I have said this before, however, as important as this is, I see no harm in saying it again.

The present time is four o'clock in the morning, and I really need another cup of coffee. While I was drinking my coffee, another thought entered my mind. If you, the reader, believe in baptismal regeneration, then you may be thinking: *If this knucklehead believes that baptism is not necessary for the remission of sins and for salvation, then why was Jesus baptized?* This is a very good question and I am so happy that you brought it up at 4 A.M.! The babbling words of a knucklehead like myself or anyone else should not have more influence on us than Scripture. Why was Jesus baptized? According to Scripture, Jesus was baptized "to fulfill all righteousness"(Mat. 3:15). However, what does to fulfill all righteousness mean?

Now Jesus himself was about thirty years old when he began his ministry. He was the son, so it was thought, of Joseph, the son of Heli,
— NIV, Luke 3:23

[13] *Then Jesus came from Galilee to the Jordan to be baptized by John.* [14] *But John tried to deter him, saying, "I need to be baptized by you, and do you come to me?"* [15] *Jesus replied, "Let it be so now; it is proper for us to do this to fulfill all righteousness." Then John consented.*
— NIV, Mat. 3:13-15

Under the Mosaic Law, Levite men at age thirty were to begin their ministry and duties pertaining to the tabernacle and later on to the Temple (Num. 4:3). This was the same age Jesus began His ministry (Luke 3:23). Also under the Mosaic Law, consecration for High Priesthood required the individual to be washed with water (Exo. 29:4). Jesus was entering His ministry and office as a priest, being washed or immersed (baptized) with water was "to fulfill all righteousness" of the Mosaic Law. Water purification for priesthood was a Jewish tradition: a requirement of the Laws of Moses. One fact which is absolutely impossible for anyone to deny is that Jesus certainly was not baptized for the remission of sins! Because there was no sin in Him (1 Pet. 2:22, 2 Cor. 5:21 and 1 John 3:5).

Realizing that Jesus was not baptized or immersed for the remission of sins, we easily see that His baptism was an act of obedience. Obedience to the Mosaic Laws which were, at that time, still binding. I understand that Jesus was baptized "to fulfill all righteousness" of the Mosaic Law. I also understand His baptism as a sign of assurance for the Jewish people. God's confirmation:

and the Holy Spirit descended on him in bodily form like a dove. And a voice came from heaven: "You are my Son, whom I love; with you I am well pleased."
— NIV, Luke 3:22

I also believe that the historical fact that Jesus did not baptize individuals (John 4:2) is also very important. His baptism signified an already-true fact or reality. His baptism was a sign, which only signified the reality that Jesus truly was the Son of God. The reality came first, then the sign, which only symbolized the reality. Abraham first heard God's Word, then he believed. Then he obeyed. Then many years later, Abraham received the physical sign of circumcision. Faith came first, then credited righteousness, then years later, "he received the sign of circumcision, a seal of the righteousness that he had by faith while he was still uncircumcised" (NIV, Rom. 4:11).

The same is true with Christians. We first hear God's Word. Then our heart is spiritually circumcised by the spiritual sword (Eph. 6:17) of the Holy Spirit.

²⁸ A man is not a Jew if he is only one outwardly, nor is circumcision merely outward and physical. ²⁹ No, a man is a Jew if he is one inwardly; and circumcision is circumcision of the heart, by the Spirit, not by the written code. Such a man's praise is not from men, but from God.

— NIV, Rom. 2:28-29

In him you were also circumcised, in the putting off of the sinful nature, not with a circumcision done by the hands of men but with the circumcision done by Christ,

— NIV, Col. 2:11

Then we believe, and because of our faith, we then obey and repent. The Holy Spirit has the ability and power and "judges the thoughts and attitudes of the heart" when we repent.

For the word of God is living and active. Sharper than any double-edged sword, it penetrates even to dividing soul and spirit, joints and marrow; it judges the thoughts and attitudes of the heart.

— NIV, Heb. 4:12

The Spirit himself testifies with our spirit that we are God's children.
— NIV, Rom. 8:16

By our personal act of repentance, we receive God's merciful forgiveness and spiritual life and also the promise and seal of the Holy Spirit. All of these blessings given by God "for" repentance. This truly is complete grace!

That the blessing of Abraham might come on the Gentiles through Jesus Christ; that we might receive the promise of the Spirit through faith
— KJV, Gal. 3:14

Repent ye therefore, and be converted, that your sins may be blotted out, when the times of refreshing shall come from the presence of the Lord;
— KJV, Acts 3:19

The Lord is not slow in keeping his promise, as some understand slowness. He is patient with you, not wanting anyone to perish, but everyone to come to repentance.
— NIV, 2 Pet. 3:9

In whom ye also trusted, after that ye heard the word of truth, the gospel of your salvation: in whom also after that ye believed, ye were sealed with that holy Spirit of promise,
— KJV, Eph. 1:13

For with the heart man believeth unto righteousness; and with the mouth confession is made unto salvation.
— KJV, Rom. 10:10

We spiritually die to our old sinful ways of living to fulfill the desires of the flesh. We spiritually crucify the old man and we are spiritually buried. Our spiritual death of our old sinful nature is only possible by our faith and our act of repentance. These realities all come first, then the physical sign, which only symbolizes these realities. Our baptism only signifies these true facts or realities. The spiritual reality is that we are a child of God, walking in His Light, and now living our new life in faith. The realities come first, then the sign, which only signifies these realities.

From our previous study of John 13:6-8, we should also now realize that Jesus used ceremonial foot washing to illustrate or to symbolize the cleansing, washing or purification which He would in the near future do by the shedding of His blood on the cross. The future spiritual washing by His blood was being symbolized by the Mosaic purification ritual of foot washing.

My understanding of baptism is that baptism is not a sacramental ritual providing remission of sins by God's grace. I understand that the remission of sin is provided by God's grace through repentance, not through baptism! Christian baptism is only an act of obedience, something a Christian is instructed to do, something a Christian should do, something a Christian should want to do. A public declaration, which symbolizes our faith in His blood for the remission of sins.

We have also studied the conversion of Cornelius and his Gentile friends. We should now realize from our previous study that these individuals were saved before water baptism. We should also realize that it is absolutely impossible for anyone to deny that these individuals were the children of God before water baptism! This undeniable truth alone should enable us to realize that remission of sin is not dependent on baptism.

* For Christ did not send me to baptize, but to preach the gospel— not with words of human wisdom, lest the cross of Christ be emptied of its power. For the message of the cross is foolishness to those who are perishing, but to us who are being saved it is the power of God.*

— NIV, 1Cor. 1:17-18

We have studied the above verses and realize that the Apostle Paul clearly states that Christ did not send him to baptize. Paul was sent to preach the gospel. Paul also informs us in these verses the reason why he was sent not to baptize: so the cross of Christ would not be emptied of its power. We should now also realize that Paul also informed the Corinthians and us that he had become their spiritual father through or by the gospel, Paul was their spiritual father and they were his spiritual children. Paul had begotten the Corinthians by preaching the Gospel, not by baptizing them.

Even though you have ten thousand guardians in Christ, you do not have many fathers, for in Christ Jesus I became your father through the gospel.

— *NIV, 1Cor. 4:15*

The Corinthians were spiritually born by faith and repentance, because of or by the spiritual sword, which Paul had preached to them. What is really important for us to realize is that Paul informs the Corinthians and us that they were baptized by the Spirit.

For we were all baptized by one Spirit into one body—whether Jews or Greeks, slave or free—and we were all given the one Spirit to drink.

— *NIV, 1Cor. 12:13*

We have studied Romans 10:10, which informs us, "For with the heart man believeth unto righteousness; and with the mouth confession is made unto salvation" (KJV).

I have heard some individuals who support baptismal regeneration theology say that, "baptism is when God does His grace thing" or "baptism is the moment when God's grace begins." I am totally unable to express with words how my heart swells with sadness and grief every time I hear those words. My understanding of Scripture is that God's merciful grace began long before the ordinance of baptism was instituted by Christ. As I was typing the word ordinance, another word came shining through the darkness of my uneducated mind. The word is Sacrament, a present moment of long personal thought, a decision to say no more!

Baptismal regeneration is a salvation dependent on:
1.   a third person (the individual who does the baptizing),
2.   the availability of water
3.   the physical ability of the individual who is baptized.

They must be physically able to enter and exit the water of regeneration. They must be physically able to be immersed "for the remission of sins" in the water of regeneration. Is this type of salvation totally dependent only on Christ? I honestly have to say: No! Is this type of salvation true to Scripture (Acts 10:43-47)? Once again, I honestly have to say: No! If you believe in baptismal regeneration then I would like you to ask yourself the following simple questions, which may be answered by a simple yes or no.

Were Cornelius and his Gentile friends Christians before water baptism? If your answer is no, then the Holy Spirit was given to the children of Satan and there is absolutely no possible way for you or anyone else to do a silly dance around this with words! I am not trying to be rude or sarcastic here. Please remember, I am only trying to get you to think of your theology. To say that Cornelius was a child of Satan filled with the Holy Spirit and speaking in tongues would be total silliness. To admit that Cornelius was a child of God before he was baptized in water would be totally destructive to your present belief and theology of baptismal regeneration. The undeniable truth according to Scripture is that Cornelius and his Gentile friends were saved before their water baptism. This historical fact is plainly stated and cannot be denied by anyone. A moment of personal thought: All I will say, is we must realize that buckets with holes never hold water!

Are we told in Romans 10:10 that with the mouth confession is made {unto: Eis} salvation? Does Acts 3:19 say that we are converted by repenting and our sins are blotted out? Are we also told in Mark 4:12 that our sins are forgiven when we are converted? Do Acts 11:18 and 2 Peter 3:9 say that repentance is for spiritual life? Does Luke 18:9-14 say that repentance brings justification? Does Ephesians 4:5 inform us that there is one Lord, one faith, one baptism? Does 1Cor. 12:13 inform us that we were all baptized by one Spirit into one body—whether Jews or Gentiles, slave or free—and we were all given the one Spirit to drink?

I am only asking you to study and only then decide for yourself. These questions are presented only in Christian love with a sincere desire for scriptural and theological harmony. If there is no harmony, then the theology must be incorrect. There is no possibility that

Scripture could be incorrect, in my mind! I hope and pray that you feel the same way about this.

I would like to remind the reader once again that the Bible plainly states that with the mouth, confession is made unto salvation (Rom. 10:10). The simplicity of this verse is a beautiful revelation to all of mankind. If we compare Romans 10:10 to Acts 3:19, Mark 4:12, Acts 11:18 and 2 Peter 3:9, we hear and see a revelation which creates a totally harmonious melody. A marvelous revelation of conversion, forgiveness and spiritual life given for repentance! Add anything to God's requirement of repentance and the result is a salvation melody of distortion. My present understanding of Scripture is that if an individual believes and repents they need nobody, except Jesus.

¹ The point of what we are saying is this: We do have such a high priest, who sat down at the right hand of the throne of the Majesty in heaven, ² and who serves in the sanctuary, the true tabernacle set up by the Lord, not by man. ³ Every high priest is appointed to offer both gifts and sacrifices, and so it was necessary for this one also to have something to offer. ⁴ If he were on earth, he would not be a priest, for there are already men who offer the gifts prescribed by the law. ⁵ They serve at a sanctuary that is a copy and shadow of what is in heaven. This is why Moses was warned when he was about to build the tabernacle: "See to it that you make everything according to the pattern shown you on the mountain." ⁶ But the ministry Jesus has received is as superior to theirs as the covenant of which he is mediator is superior to the old one, and it is founded on better promises. ⁷ For if there had been nothing wrong with that first covenant, no place would have been sought for another. ⁸ But God found fault with the people and said : "The time is coming, declares the Lord, when I will make a new covenant with the house of Israel and with the house of Judah. ⁹ It will not be like the covenant I made with their forefathers when I took them by the hand to lead them out of Egypt, because they did not remain faithful to my covenant, and I turned away from them, declares the Lord. ¹⁰ This is the covenant I will make with the house of Israel after that time, declares the

Lord. I will put my laws in their minds and write them on their hearts. I will be their God, and they will be my people. [11] No longer will a man teach his neighbor, or a man his brother, saying, 'Know the Lord,' because they will all know me, from the least of them to the greatest [12] For I will forgive their wickedness and will remember their sins no more" [13] By calling this covenant "new," he has made the first one obsolete; and what is obsolete and aging will soon disappear.

— NIV, Heb. 8:1-13

[1] Now the first covenant had regulations for worship and also an earthly sanctuary. [2] A tabernacle was set up. In its first room were the lampstand, the table and the consecrated bread; this was called the Holy Place. [3] Behind the second curtain was a room called the Most Holy Place, [4] which had the golden altar of incense and the gold-covered ark of the covenant. This ark contained the gold jar of manna, Aaron's staff that had budded, and the stone tablets of the covenant. [5] Above the ark were the cherubim of the Glory, overshadowing the atonement cover. But we cannot discuss these things in detail now. [6] When everything had been arranged like this, the priests entered regularly into the outer room to carry on their ministry. [7] But only the high priest entered the inner room, and that only once a year, and never without blood, which he offered for himself and for the sins the people had committed in ignorance. [8] The Holy Spirit was showing by this that the way into the Most Holy Place had not yet been disclosed as long as the first tabernacle was still standing. [9] This is an illustration for the present time, indicating that the gifts and sacrifices being offered were not able to clear the conscience of the worshiper. [10] They are only a matter of food and drink and various ceremonial washings—external regulations applying until the time of the new order. [11] When Christ came as high priest of the good things that are already here, he went through the greater and more perfect tabernacle that is not man-made, that is to say, not a part of this creation. [12] He did not enter by means of the blood of goats and calves; but he entered the

Most Holy Place once for all by his own blood, having obtained eternal redemption.

— NIV, Heb. 9:1-12

[19] *Therefore, brothers, since we have confidence to enter the Most Holy Place by the blood of Jesus,* [20] *by a new and living way opened for us through the curtain, that is, his body,* [21] *and since we have a great priest over the house of God,* [22] *let us draw near to God with a sincere heart in full assurance of faith, having our hearts sprinkled to cleanse us from a guilty conscience and having our bodies washed with pure water.*

— NIV, Heb. 10:19-22

In him and through faith in him we may approach God with freedom and confidence.

— NIV, Eph. 3:12

Sacramental rituals for atonement are now obsolete and were discontinued. The Lamb of God was a sacrifice of atonement through faith in His blood for the remission of sins. He was an eternal sacrifice: for redemption, a new High Priest and a new covenant.

This is my blood of the covenant, which is poured out for many for the forgiveness of sins.

— NIV, Mat. 26:28

God presented him as a sacrifice of atonement, through faith in his blood. He did this to demonstrate his justice, because in his forbearance he had left the sins committed beforehand unpunished

— NIV, Rom. 3:25

For there is one God and one mediator between God and men, the man Christ Jesus,

— NIV, 1Tim. 2:5

Chapter 16

Christian Unity

I stated in the beginning of this book that I personally do not believe that any individual Christian or any individual Christian denomination has a completely correct understanding of all Scripture. If you, the reader, understand baptismal regeneration to be Christian conversion and if you personally only recognize individuals who have been baptized literally to receive the forgiveness of sins, as Christians, what more could I say or do? I only ask you to do what I will continue to do, pray and study God's written word. As for my family and myself, we consider you to be a Christian brother or sister in Christ. I sincerely hope and pray that you have the same opinion of me. In my mind and in my heart and soul, I truly believe that anyone who has repented and who confesses Jesus to be their Lord and Savior is a child of God.

I believe that Christian unity is only possible when we deliberately refuse to accept any manmade creed which create walls of division. Creeds, which lead only to hostility and eventually to total separation, should have no place in Christianity. The necessity of manmade creeds is a result of the reality of the imperfect state of man and the imperfect state of the physical world in which we live. This necessity of creeds should extend only to the necessary guidelines needed for Christian fellowship and worship. They should never be created nor should they ever be used as destructive weapons of exclusion and bigotry. Bigotry and non-recognition of others are common traits of cults and should never be permitted or tolerated in any Christian denomination. I am a member of the Church of the Nazarene; however, the members of this denomination are not the only

Christians. If any Christian denomination should believe that they are the only Christians, then that denomination in reality is nothing more than a cult and has no place in Christianity!

Each one of us are to walk and witness with the present spiritual light which has been given to us. We should be working together towards harmony with a never-ending hunger and a continuously growing desire, filling our hearts and creating a striving united force of Christian love and unity of all believers. I believe in my heart and soul that there will be no place in Heaven for denominational walls. We should realize that the body of Christ has many different denominational members and together each of these individual members are only a part of the whole: His spiritual church. If we fail individually to mature spiritually, we live and suffer the losses from our immaturity. However, His spiritual church as a whole is then forced to live and suffer also from the losses of our immaturity.

Christians of all denominations should realize that the strength of His spiritual church as a whole is dependent on the continuous spiritual growth of each individual Christian. Our prayers should be for the spiritual maturity of all Christians and the unity our maturity would bring to and for all Christian denominations. This Christian unity would give Christianity the spiritual fruit of strength, for all Christians and for all Christian denominations. The greater the unity becomes, the stronger Christianity becomes. The stronger Christianity becomes, the greater the numbers will be who will glorify nobody, except Jesus!

Unity is no different than anything else in life; there must be a starting point. Two thousand years past the crucifixion of Christ, Christians, who believe and serve the same God, sadly have different ways of receiving His forgiveness and grace. If unity truly is our common goal, then we must come to an agreement on the requirements for Christian conversion. *NoBODY, except JESUS* is my small effort towards this goal. For centuries men have debated these requirements. If this first step towards unity is never taken, then unity will never become a reality. This is only one reason why our spiritual maturity is so important; unity will only be a possibility when individuals study God's written word and stop believing what someone else is telling them to be true to God's written word.

Spiritual maturity and discernment are only possible when we have taken the time to study God's written word. The more we study, the more understanding we receive. The more we understand, the closer we should be to agreement on what constitutes scriptural Christian conversion. The more we understand, the harder it becomes to be deceived. To be perfectly honest with you and to get right to the point, what I am saying is that laziness will never receive anything of value, nor will it take us any closer to unity. If we do not study, then we will continue to believe whatever we are told by others. Unity requires agreement, agreement requires discernment, discernment requires knowledge and knowledge is only possible when efforts have been made to understand spiritual truths. Discernment is a God given responsibility to and for all Christians. Aside from salvation, I honestly believe that the spiritual maturity of Christians should be the priority of all Christian denominations.

[12] *In fact, though by this time you ought to be teachers, you need someone to teach you the elementary truths of God's word all over again. You need milk, not solid food!* [13] *Anyone who lives on milk, being still an infant, is not acquainted with the teaching about righteousness.* [14] *But solid food is for the mature, who by constant use have trained themselves to distinguish good from evil.*
— *NIV, Heb. 5:12-14*

You must teach what is in accord with sound doctrine.
— *NIV, Titus 2:1*

[16] *All Scripture is God-breathed and is useful for teaching, rebuking, correcting and training in righteousness,* [17] *so that the man of God may be thoroughly equipped for every good work.*
— *NIV, 2 Tim. 3:16-17*

Preach the Word; be prepared in season and out of season; correct, rebuke and encourage—with great patience and careful instruction.
— *NIV, 2 Tim. 4:2*

We should not place these responsibilities on others, believing that this responsibility is only for those who are ministers or Sunday school teachers. In my opinion, this type of thinking is nothing more than an attempt to justify our acts of irresponsibility and our personal state of laziness. I believe the reasoning for this way of thinking, is by placing the responsibility on someone else, conviction and guilt then, can never become a possible reality in our hearts or in our minds. This may very well be true. However, if we realize that the Holy Spirit uses guilt to convict the world of sin (John 16:8 NIV), we then remember that guilt played a very important role in our conversion. Guilt was the element which brought us to conviction; guilt and conviction led us to repentance. Just as the Holy Spirit used guilt to lead us to repentance, guilt is also used by the Spirit to encourage us to make changes and mature spiritually. Removing this responsibility also eliminates guilt, eliminate guilt and the Holy Spirit's power to convict is weakened.

Guilt is not only a very important element leading us to repentance, guilt is also very important to our continuous spiritual maturity and growth. We should never do anything which may work against the workings of the Holy Spirit. We are to be led by the Spirit (Rom. 8:14).We should never be working against the Spirit nor should we be attempting to bind the Spirit in anyway. Guilt is very beneficial to man; guilt causes individuals to examine their actions and this in turn can motivate and bring positive changes. If we feel guilt, we should be honestly asking ourselves why. If the reason or cause of our guilt is due to our laziness and our lack of efforts to grow spiritually, or to sin, then guilt is providing us with a spiritual warning which we should listen to and heed. I truly believe that the involvement of the Holy Spirit in the life of a Christian should never be ignored nor should we underestimate the power of the Spirit.

Is unity nothing more than the desire of man, dreaming in his unrealistic mind, fueled by the burning flames of love, residing in his converted heart of flesh? Is total Christian unity possible? I honestly have to say that I personally do not believe so. I would be willing to say that this statement may have surprised you. You may even be asking yourself, *then why is this nitwit writing about Christian unity, if he does not believe it is possible?* I will try to explain why.

[11] It was he who gave some to be apostles, some to be prophets, some to be evangelists, and some to be pastors and teachers, [12] to prepare God's people for works of service, so that the body of Christ may be built up [13] until we all reach unity in the faith and in the knowledge of the Son of God and become mature, attaining to the whole measure of the fullness of Christ. [14] Then we will no longer be infants, tossed back and forth by the waves, and blown here and there by every wind of teaching and by the cunning and craftiness of men in their deceitful scheming. [15] Instead, speaking the truth in love, we will in all things grow up into him who is the Head, that is, Christ. [16] From him the whole body, joined and held together by every supporting ligament, grows and builds itself up in love, as each part does its work.

— NIV, Eph. 4:11-16

We are instructed to "become mature, attaining to the whole measure of the fullness of Christ." The "fullness of Christ" means the perfection of Christ. The perfection of Christ means without sin, holiness to divine perfection, totally sinless, the righteousness or the fullness of Christ. I also personally do not believe that it is possible for any Christian, let alone all Christians, to achieve this fullness of Christ in this life. What I believe is not important; what is important is what God has instructed us to do in His written word. We are instructed to work for unity and also to attain the fullness of Christ. The key words in this verse are "until we all reach" "unity in the faith" "and the fullness of Christ." The righteousness of Christ could never be achieved by any man's obedience to the law.

"I do not set aside the grace of God, for if righteousness could be gained through the law, Christ died for nothing!"

— NIV, Gal 2:21

Realizing that we will never in this life achieve the righteousness or the fullness of Christ does not change the fact that we are instructed by God's written word to continuously work towards these two goals "until we all reach unity in the faith and in the knowledge of the Son of God and become mature, attaining to the whole measure of the fullness of Christ." We are instructed to continuously work towards these goals our entire life, "until we all reach" these goals! It does not matter what I think or what you may think, our opinions do not change the biblical truth that these inspired instructions are from God. I am writing about Christian unity and Christian maturity ("the fullness of Christ" Eph. 4:13) because God has instructed all of us to continuously work towards these goals. Christian unity being an inspired instruction from God is then the responsibility of all Christians. Denominational names may always exist in this present physical world of ours, however, this does not mean that the differences in their theology have to remain as diversified as they presently are.

Almost two thousand years past the crucifixion of Christ, denominations of Christianity have been unable to come to an agreement on the first step towards Christian unity, which is what does Scripture require for Christian conversion? What are we doing wrong? Is this issue of theology that complicated and that far beyond man's intellectual ability? Or have we just been too busy to obey God's instructions concerning unity? Have man-written creeds and the pride of men prevented changes in denominational creeds? Changes, which could narrow the theological differences between denominations! Could man-written creeds, some unchanged for hundreds of years, and the pride of men who refuse to admit to their incorrect theology because they believe that these creeds were written in stone, be partly responsible? Could the laziness and passivity of Christians also be partly responsible? I am not trying to start a revolution in Christianity, I am only pleading for spiritual maturity and only for corrective theological changes in man-written creeds. I personally know many Christians who have told me that they do not agree with the theological doctrine of their Church, yet they continue to worship, serve and support their denominational Church, even without expressing their oppositions.

You must teach what is in accord with sound doctrine.
— NIV, Titus 2:1

Preach the Word; be prepared in season and out of season; correct, rebuke and encourage—with great patience and careful instruction.

— *NIV, 2 Tim. 4:2*

I realize that the majority of us do not like change; however, in my opinion, this does not justify our passivity nor will it remove or eliminate our accountability. One of the most difficult things I have ever had to do was to leave a Church where I had worshipped, served and supported for ten years. I truly did not want to leave this Church. I realized that I could not let my desires and emotions influence the right I knew. The decision was either do what I wanted to do, or do what I believed God wanted me to do. Once I looked at it this way, no longer was there a decision to be made.

Christian churches, attempting to attract and please the majority, have continuously made changes in music and in worship services. The goal of these changes being to increase numerical growth, ensuring their survival. These changes are rarely made without some level of opposition. The leadership of these churches make these changes because they realize that these changes are necessary because of our changing society. If people don't like our music, they will not come back. If they don't come back, then our church will not survive; it is that simple. These changes are made because society will not tolerate anything that society does not want. The point, which I am trying to bring to light here, is that IF Christians viewed their spiritual maturity seriously, our understanding of spiritual truth would increase; this would either enable changes to be made in man-written denominational creeds or a change where we worship and serve. Either one of these changes, in my opinion, would be a step towards unity.

Positive changes necessary for any desired goal are never made without an initial cost of some kind. This should never prevent changes for the good from being made. We must someday seriously face the historical fact that Christianity has failed to agree on what constitutes Christian conversion. The reality of this historical fact should be a wake-up call for all denominations. This shameful historical fact should motivate every single Christian on the planet to do something. I wonder and have asked myself many times: what message is this never-ending controversy giving to mankind? Christianity says there is one God; however, Christianity is unable to agree on what constitutes Christian conversion. If this is not a pitiful state to be in, after almost two thousand years past the crucifixion, I am really unable to imagine anything more pitiful.

I am sure that you have heard the saying "united we stand, divided we fall." Could the dark satanic forces of evil and the Master of lies be at work preventing unity among Christian denominations? Could the lack of unity and the division of Christians be a deliberate strategic plan of a desperate spiritual foe? Could our laziness and our lack of concern for unity and maturity weaken Christianity? If we take time to think about the present condition of the Church, we may soon realize that as time marches on, the Church seems to be growing weaker with every new generation. Most congregations today have a small number of committed individuals who are willing to serve. This may not seem to be very important until we realize that this is causing additional work for these individuals. Additional work requires the sacrifice of additional energy and time. The loss of this additional time can be very costly. Time, which could have been used to study God's word, time which could have been time for nourishment, which is necessary for growth and maturity. Satan is evil, deceitful and desperate; however, Satan is not stupid.

I am forced to ask myself, will Christianity decline because we lack Christian unity and agreement on what constitutes Christian conversion? Could our state of personal passivity contribute to the decline in Christianity? Will our lack of individual commitment to spiritual growth contribute to the number of individuals who never personally accept Jesus as their Lord and Savior? Will our own children or perhaps our grandchildren also be one of these unfortunate individuals?! We have absolutely no control over the past, we do have control of what we do today, and what we do today will have a great influence on the future state of Christianity and our future unavoidable day of accountability before the heavenly throne. I do not know what words you hope to hear on this glorious future day. I pray that all of us will hear (Mat 25:21). Realizing Christian unity is a God given responsibility is a necessity for all Christians. This should then motivate us to continuously strive towards this common goal.

I remember a time in my life when I sincerely believed that there was just no time to study God's word. I began to feel the spiritual prick of guilt in my heart and praised the Holy Spirit for this conviction. I thought about this problem and I decided a solution would be to get a set of audiocassette tapes of the Bible. Listening to these tapes while driving filled my heart with a stronger desire to study. In a very short time, I found myself making time to study God's word. The more I studied, the greater the desire became to study even more. This was not a miracle; it was only an example of the power of God's word and the ability of the Spirit to bring conviction to the heart and mind of a simple man. The days were not any longer nor did my other responsibilities become fewer, the only thing that had changed was my desire and my priorities. My increased desire and the change of my priorities resulted from the guilt filling my heart and mind, which had been brought or given to me by the workings of the Holy Spirit. The Holy Spirit was guiding and teaching; however, I had to make a personal decision to listen and yield to his guidance or to ignore this spiritual warning and continue on my spiritual walk in life being lead by the carnal mind of the flesh. The Spirit is willing to guide, the mind of man must decide to yield and follow. The reality of this is true for all Christians.

Have you ever thought about what you might believe today if different parents had raised you? Our thinking and what we believe are greatly influenced by our early years of life. These early years of life are probably the most impressionable years of our lives. I personally have friends who believe exactly what their parents believe, without ever having taken the time to personally study Scripture for themselves. I believe this is increasing in our present society among many Christians. This type of discipleship is a very serious problem today in Christianity and could become even a greater problem for the Church in the future. The lifestyles we have today demand so much of our energy and time. Many times we feel that there are just not enough hours in a day. We are running here and running there, just trying to keep up with the daily routine of our busy lives and our responsibilities. No time to do this, no time to do that, no time for me and no time for God! Some Christians may honestly believe that they just have no time to study God's word. Honestly believing this does not make it right. Both our time and our energy are given to our priorities. In my mind, our responsibility of spiritual maturity and discernment should be at the very top of our priority list.

When I think of the Apostle Paul, I realize that almost two thousand years ago, Paul was faced with the same problems of discernment and unity. At an early age, Paul had been sent by his parents to be taught by Gamaliel (Acts 22:3) who was a great Jewish rabbi (teacher) of the first century. Paul had been raised by his parents and greatly influenced by their beliefs in traditional Judaism, which his parents believed to be spiritual truths. Likewise, we also are raised and taught to believe the traditional beliefs of our parents. It has probably always been this way and more than likely it will always continue to be this way.

Paul was a Hebrew among Hebrew men (Phil. 3:5), a Roman citizen, a Pharisee, a man who was respected, honored, and also a man of power. A man whose heart and mind were filled with love and devotion for God and the traditional Laws of Moses, which had been taught to him since his early childhood. A love for his God so powerful that this same love gave birth to his hatred for Christians. A love for his God drove and motivated his determination to hunt and persecute all Christians, both men and women. All of his natural senses could not tolerate anything to do with Christianity or a crucified man named Jesus. Paul's ears, eyes, mind and heart were completely spiritually dead. A devoted Jewish Pharisee who was physically circumcised (Phil. 3:5) however not yet spiritually circumcised in his heart (Rom. 2:28-29). A sincerely devoted individual, who was unable to discern spiritual truths. Paul had believed that his mission of Christian persecution was an act of righteousness, motivated by his love for God. Paul was living his life believing the incorrect things, which had been taught to him. He was an individual devoted to God who was actually persecuting God, because of the total spiritual blindness of his educated and intellectual mind. He was a devoted and God-fearing man walking in total spiritual darkness.

⁹ "I too was convinced that I ought to do all that was possible to oppose the name of Jesus of Nazareth. ¹⁰ And that is just what I did in Jerusalem. On the authority of the chief priests I put many of the saints in prison, and when they were put to death, I cast my vote against them. ¹¹ Many a time I went from one synagogue to another to have them punished, and I tried to force them to blaspheme. In my obsession against them, I even went to foreign cities to persecute them."

— *NIV, Acts 26:9-11*

I think that it would be reasonable to say that, beyond Satan himself, Paul was probably the greatest physical enemy and persecutor of the Church in his day, before his conversion on the road to Damascus. It may be very easy for some of us to realize how difficult it would have been for a man like Paul to abandon his strict religious training and upbringing. Could a sincere incorrect understanding of spiritual truths along with devotion and love for God actually do more harm than good? In my opinion, it certainly did in Paul's case. I truly believe that all individuals should always keep an open mind to our present understanding of Scripture. We should never believe just because we have been told what to believe. We should study and only then decide what we believe. Before Paul saw the Light on that road to Damascus, he was totally convinced that his way of religious beliefs (Judaism) were right and true to God's word. He was a man totally committed to God, walking through life in the spiritual darkness of his incorrect religious upbringing. Could this also be true for some of us today?

The following verses apply to all Christians in one way or another. When we read and study these verses, a feeling of assurance giving peace are felt from within, or a feeling of....?

¹⁶ All Scripture is God-breathed and is useful for teaching, rebuking, correcting and training in righteousness, ¹⁷ so that the man of God may be thoroughly equipped for every good work.

— *NIV, 2 Tim. 3:16-17*

Preach the Word; be prepared in season and out of season; correct, rebuke and encourage—with great patience and careful instruction.

— NIV, 2 Tim. 4:2

[12] In fact, though by this time you ought to be teachers, you need someone to teach you the elementary truths of God's word all over again. You need milk, not solid food! [13] Anyone who lives on milk, being still an infant, is not acquainted with the teaching about righteousness. [14] But solid food is for the mature, who by constant use have trained themselves to distinguish good from evil.

— NIV, Heb. 5:12-14

[1] Therefore let us leave the elementary teachings about Christ and go on to maturity, not laying again the foundation of repentance from acts that lead to death, and of faith in God, [2] instruction about baptisms, the laying on of hands, the resurrection of the dead, and eternal judgment.

— NIV, Heb. 6:1-2

In the above two verses (Heb. 6:1-2), (1) the teachings about Christ, (2) the necessity of repentance of sins, (3) faith in God, (4) instruction about baptisms, (5) the laying on of hands, (6) the resurrection of the dead and (7) eternal judgment, are all described as elementary teachings which we are instructed to move beyond. In others words, we are instructed to come to agreement on these elementary teachings, and then we are also instructed to go on to spiritual maturity, leaving these basics. Unity is not possible without agreement and agreement still seems so far away. You may be thinking that the spiritual maturity of Christians will not bring denominational Christianity any closer to agreement and unity. You may be right. Let's assume that you are right about this. Even if the spiritual maturity of Christians did not bring Christianity any closer to unity, would the spiritual maturity of Christians be beneficial to Christianity and the spiritual body of Christ? Would the spiritual maturity of Christians be something bad? It really does not matter if you or I believe that unity is possible or not possible. What really matters is the biblical truth that unity and maturity are God given instructions for all Christians.

God presented him as a sacrifice of atonement, through faith in his blood. He did this to demonstrate his justice, because in his forbearance he had left the sins committed beforehand unpunished

— NIV, Rom. 3:25

In him and through faith in him we may approach God with freedom and confidence.

— NIV, Eph. 3:12

[20] by a new and living way opened for us through the curtain, that is, his body, [21] and since we have a great priest over the house of God, [22] let us draw near to God with a sincere heart in full assurance of faith, having our hearts sprinkled to cleanse us from a guilty conscience and having our bodies washed with pure water.

— Heb. 10:20-22

In him we have redemption through his blood, the forgiveness of sins, in accordance with the riches of God's grace.

— NIV, Eph. 1:7

God exalted him to his own right hand as Prince and Savior that he might give repentance and forgiveness of sins to Israel.

— NIV, Acts 5:31

I hope that you have enjoyed reading this book. I sincerely hope that you have also prayed and studied Scripture while reading this book. My desire has been to provide accurate information. My prayers are for all Christians to study God's written Word and only then decide for themselves what is spiritual truth. Within Scripture, we have an undeniable recorded historical account of conversion before water baptism. The undeniable truth is that we are converted and given spiritual life by the act of repentance (Mark 4:12, Acts 3:19, Acts 11:18, Rom. 10:10 & 2 Pet. 3:9) not by the act of water baptism. As Christians, we have the responsibility of spiritual maturity and discernment. Please study! Fulfilling these responsibilities is dependent on our commitment to Christ and where we place our priorities and time. I pray that I have presented God's gracious merciful unmerited forgiveness and the simplicity of conversion accurately and according to Scripture.

I thank you once again, and may God richly bless you!

The Lord is not slow in keeping his promise, as some understand slowness. He is patient with you, not wanting anyone to perish, but everyone to come to repentance.

— *NIV, 2 Pet. 3:9*

For it is with your heart that you believe and are justified, and it is with your mouth that you confess and are saved.

— *Rom. 10:10*

Endnotes

Chapter 1

[i]   Strong's Greek and Hebrew Concordance
G26. agape, ag-ah'-pay; from G25; love, i.e.
affection or benevolence; spec. (plur.) a love-
feast:—(feast of) charity ([-ably]), dear, love.

Chapter 2

[i]   Informational Web sites for: Jewish Baptisms and
Mikvah.
(1) www.aihls.org/baptism.html
(2) www.haydid.org/ronimmer.htm
(3) www.remnant.net/baptism.htm

Chapter 5

[i]   "Amazing Grace" by John Newton (1725 - 1807).

Chapter 6

[i]   Please compare this verse (Acts 11:16) with the
following verses: Rom. 8:16, Rom. 15:16, Gal. 3:14,
1Cor. 12:13, 2Cor. 1:21-22, Eph. 1:12-14 and Eph.
4:4-5

[ii]   "unto" Translated from the same Greek preposition
"eis," which is also in Acts 2:38

Chapter 9

[i]   "toward" translated from the same Greek
preposition, "eis," which is also found in Acts 2:38

Chapter 12

[i]   1831 *The Millennial Harbinger*: Pg. 481.

[ii]   1823 *The Campbell-McCalla Debate*: Pg. 135.

[iii]   1829 *The Christian Baptist*: Pg. 521.

[iv]   1843 *The Campbell-Rice Debate*: Pg. 472

[v]   *The Christian System*, 2d. Ed. (1839) Pg. 7 & 8.

[vi]   *The Christian Baptist* (1889 Edition) Volume 6, "The Three Kingdoms" by Alexander Campbell: Pg. 557-558.

Web Site: http://www.mun.ca/rels/restmov/texts/ acampbell/tcb/TCB611.HTM

[vii]   "understood in the present day" 1829.